ERRATUM

On Page 2 of *The Welfare of My Neighbor: Living out Christ's Love for the Poor*, three lines were inadvertently left off. Herein lies the paragraph in its entirety.

D1456452

FAMILY RESEARCH COUNCIL
801 G Street, N.W.
Washington, D.C. 20001

1-800-225-4008
www.frc.org

The Welfare of My Neighbor

Living Out Christ's Love for the Poor

To my mother, Grace, who has taught me more about God's grace than anyone else I know, and to my father, David, who has demonstrated the love of the Father to me in countless practical ways.

The Welfare of My Neighbor: Living Out Christ's Love for the Poor
Copyright 1999 © by Family Research Council.

Published by Family Research Council
801 G Street, NW, Washington, DC 20001

Printed in the United States of America.
Library of Congress Catalog Card Number 99-074542
ISBN 1-55872-002-2

Unless otherwise noted, Bible quotations are from the New International Version.

Cover Image: © Slocum-Quinn. "The Banquet," 1997. Used by permission.
The painting depicts Monday lunch at the "Southeast White House" in Washington, D.C. Also affectionately known as "the Little White House," this Christ-centered ministry house sits on Pennsylvania Ave., SE (in a low-income neighborhood called Anacostia). There,

Contents

Acknowledgments

Without you, God, this work would not have been possible. Thank You for continuing to decrease us so you might increase. You remain true to Your Word, Lord. All glory to You, alone.

Thank you, Family Research Council, for your support of this project. Particularly, I thank Chuck Donovan for his insight, patience and belief in me as I worked on these pages. Thank you to the wonderful team at FRC: Gina Dalfonzo, senior editor, and Leslie Carbone for your detailed edits, Amy Fox, art director, and Ashleigh Ruther for your graphic design work, Erica Pinkston and Nick Cirmo for your marketing help, Tom Atwood for your comments, and Alane McCotter for your administrative help. I was blessed with a conscientious cadre of Witherspoon Fellows who provided invaluable research and writing assistance along the way: Jeannie Callahan, Missy Negri, Marie Rapier, Gabriela Fernandez, Heidi Schneringer, and Amy Smith. Thank you.

Thank you, Debbie Stafford, director of development for at Project Heritage, for getting this project off the ground, literally. You flew to Washington, D.C., twice to write these pages with me. Their contents are a reflection of your thoughts, insights, and expertise from your personal experiences and church-based work through Project Heritage. Thank you for co-laboring with me for many months and for your close review at all stages.

Thank you to the many colleagues across the country who provided insights, mentoring and support to me. Thank you, Bill Mattox, for bringing me to FRC, and you, Jennifer E. Marshall, for initiating this work through FRC. Others I must thank include Clark and Edith Jones and Vision D.C.; Mike Herman and Calvary Baptist Church, Compton, Calif.; H. Spees and the Fresno Leadership Foundation; John Perkins and the Christian Community Development Association; William Haley and the D.C. Emerging Urban Leaders Network; David Lawson and the Urban Alternative; Step of Richmond, Va.; North American Association of Christians in Social Work; Margaret Struder; Dr. Corinthia Boone; Paget Rhee; Pastor Bob

Mathieu; David and Delmarie Hines; Dave Thompson; Steve Fitzhugh; Randy White; Virgil Gulker; Jerald January; Dr. and Mrs. Edward Eyring; Pat Mahoney; Steve Morgan; Dr. T. Victor Erekosima; Pastor Leon Lipscombe, Sr.; and Steve Park.

Thank you, also, to the Christian laborers for welfare families who have encouraged and inspired me, particularly Kevin Bradley, Dan Dyer, Amy Sherman, Bill Raymond, and Stanley Carlson-Thies.

Thank you to Robert Rector and Sarah Youssef of the Heritage Foundation and Tom Riley's team at Statistical Assessment Service for research help.

I have been blessed with a support group of friends who understood the weight of this project and carried me at points. You not only loved me but also challenged me to a deeper knowledge of God through your lives. Thank you, Anne Dickey, Chin-Chin Ip, Anthony Stacy, Ed and Karen Moy, Debbie Wong, Susan Ashcraft, and Capitol Hill Baptist Church. I am deeply indebted to my family in California and to Auntie Ruth and the ladies at Crown Pointe Retirement Center for your prayers.

My deepest thanks to the reviewers:

Stanley Carlson-Thies, director of Social Policy Studies, Center for Public Justice in Annapolis, Md.

The Reverend Samuel Harrell, director of Community Impact Institute, Center for Urban Resources in Philadelphia, Pa.

Debbie Stafford, director of development for Project Heritage and associate pastor of Heritage Christian Center in Denver, Colo.

Dave Treadwell, executive director, Central Union Mission in Washington, D.C.

Preface

by Debbie Stafford

never dreamed that I would end up on welfare with three small children 15 years ago. As a pastor's wife, I thought that I would live the rest of my life as a wife and mother. Loving my family and the people in our congregation was all that mattered to me. After 10 years of marriage, however, I experienced a traumatic divorce that left me devastated and hopeless. I was in such shock that I could barely put one foot in front of the other.

The day that I had to apply for welfare and have my picture taken for my I.D. was one of the saddest days of my life. I wondered how on earth I would ever get out of the pit that I found myself in.

While my family and I were on welfare, I knew that people in churches wanted to help us. However, I think it was difficult for people to know what to say or do. It felt like the awkwardness that seems to accompany the uncertain response to death.

Then a man from another church in our community began to train me to sell life insurance. I was in such a fog that I did everything he told me to do. If he said I needed 10 appointments in one week and had to close four sales, I did that. Within seven months I became a regional vice president in his company. I worked my way off welfare on 100 percent commission sales in just less than a year.

As I have healed and moved on with my life, I believe that God has given me a charge to help churches create practical ministries to touch people in need. I now know there are millions of families who are trapped in welfare dependency and need a way out, just as I did. Due to the new welfare reforms of 1996, welfare families are losing their benefits. Many are also losing hope in God and His church.

The choice to help our neighbor off welfare is up to each one of us. This book provides education and resources to assist your church in helping a family like mine. I am convinced that no matter its size or location, every church in America could do more than it currently is doing for a welfare family. In this critical hour, the future of some of the neediest families in the United States awaits our response.

Debbie Stafford is an associate pastor on the staff of Heritage Christian Center and the director of development for Project Heritage, a ministry to welfare families, in Denver, Colo. She is co-author of the book *Shattered Dreams: A Biblical Outlook on Domestic Violence*. She has also adapted the Denver Police Department's *Victim's Handbook on Domestic Violence* to reflect a biblical perspective. Debbie is a strong voice for challenging churches to respond to the new needs caused by welfare reform. She and her husband, Tom, have a blended family of five children and seven grandchildren and live in Denver.

Introduction

T his book had its beginnings before I started to understand what poverty was, and even before I truly knew what being a Christian was. I remember seeing the images of poverty on TV when I was a child. "If you will send us money, you will help eliminate poverty," was how the commercial would usually end. My first glimpse of distressing human need was of faraway countries where children were starving. It troubled me that children would go to bed at night without food.

I became a Christian when I was five, but it was not until the eighth grade that my eyes really opened to the needs around me. Jesus tells us that the second greatest commandment is to "love one's neighbor as oneself." I first thought *neighbor* meant just those people that I encountered through my normal routine. Most of those people were like me. We had the same skin color, the same zip code, and the same lifestyle. Many of us went to the same church.

When I was in seventh grade, however, my family changed churches. My new youth pastor, Doug Haag, had a deep passion and conviction for helping others. He encouraged me to go with our junior high youth group to serve in Mexico when I was in eighth grade.

From our southern California church, Mexico was just a short drive over the border in the church bus. Yet I returned home from that trip changed. I had a new idea of whom Jesus meant when he said, "Love your neighbor as yourself."

In the years following, my definition of *neighbor* changed to include those "nearby" (from the Greek word for neighbor, *plesion*) who had different ethnicities, cultures, and even languages. God started showing me that He meant me to love those in my community and nearby city who had very practical needs such as food, clothing, and shelter. There was no mistaking that God's heart for outreach included relating to those who were different from me.

This book was born out of the conviction that God desires the Christian community to love our neighbors in practical, as well as spiritual, ways. Specifically, God desires His church to have a tender affection and yearning for our neighbors who are in need (as the Greek word for *compassion, spagchnon*, implies). This tenderness is specific in its objects: the orphan, the widow, the prisoner, the alien, and the dispossessed, in the United States and around the world. This book has as its focus our needy families in the United States who are on, or have recently escaped, government welfare.

One of Jesus' best-known stories begins with a Jewish attorney asking Jesus, "Teacher, what must I do to inherit eternal life?" Jesus' reply is, "Love your neighbor as yourself." When the attorney asks, "Who is my neighbor?" Jesus tells him the story of the Good Samaritan.

This book attempts to help the church fulfill Jesus' command to "love your neighbor as yourself" and to answer the attorney's question within a practical context in the United States. It will bring the idea of *neighbor*, specifically our poor neighbors on government welfare, into clearer view. We will see that these neighbors are facing special challenges right now due to a major change in the law, and that the church has a pivotal role in their transformation.

How, then, do we love our neighbors? I met a Christian man a few months ago who captured the sentiment of many Christians toward those who are poor. He said, "My wife and I care. We just don't know what to do." Those who will benefit most from this book are those Christians who want to love others but, like this couple, don't know what to do. This book is also designed for pastors and lay leaders seeking to bring their congregations outside the walls of their churches to minister among the poor in their neighborhood and in the city.

Ministry leaders, missions pastors, and practitioners will find the resources in Part 2 particularly helpful. Several innovative books and ministries that can help your church expand its current outreach efforts in the community are presented. In the appendix, you will find specific information about policy changes and funding opportunities for churches that have developed from the welfare reform legislation of 1996.

Social workers like myself must reorient social work to its Christian, community-organizing roots. I hope this work is part of the beginning of a collection of writings in which we take our experience with the poor and translate it into practical education for church-based outreach in America. This reorientation means our biblical beliefs will inform our social work practice, and we will subsequently regard the church as a distinct organism in our communities.

The outreach ministries of our churches are in a time of transition. Through welfare reform, America's landscape for helping the poor is changing quickly. It isn't just about churches giving away canned goods or motel vouchers anymore. Welfare families need to be equipped to move to a place of independence and self-sufficiency. They need new life — and churches can help them find it. There is so much good work to do.

Deanna Lynn Carlson
Washington, D.C.
December 1998

Part 1

KNOWING MY NEIGHBOR

The following pages will introduce you to your neighbors who are on or have recently left welfare. Made in God's image, these neighbors who are visibly needy have so much to teach each one of us about Him. Loving our poor neighbors begins with knowing them – each with a name, a story, and dreams for the future.

"A man was going down from Jerusalem to Jericho, when he fell into the hands of robbers. They stripped him of his clothes, beat him and went away, leaving him half dead. A priest happened to be going down the same road, and when he saw the man, he passed by on the other side. So too, a Levite, when he came to the place and saw him, passed by on the other side. But a Samaritan, as he traveled, came where the man was; and when he saw him he took pity on him. He went to him pouring on oil and wine. Then he put the man on his own donkey, took him to an inn and took care of him. The next day he took out two silver coins and gave them to the innkeeper. 'Look after him,' he said, 'and when I return, I will reimburse you for any extra expense you may have.'" (Luke 10:30-35)

Chapter One

WHO IS MY POOR NEIGHBOR?

He who despises his neighbors sins, but happy is he who is gracious to the poor.
Proverbs 14:20b (NASB)

The biggest disease today is not leprosy or tuberculosis, but rather the feeling of being unwanted, uncared for and deserted by everybody.
Mother Teresa[1]

Tommy lived only five miles away from me, but we could have been countries apart. The only reason that I met him was that I was his social worker. He did not have any family support; he had a hard time holding a job because he was disabled; and he had a history of self-defeating behaviors.

Tommy's situation, after just a few months of my doing home visits in the community, started to become familiar. I soon realized how many despairing people lived in my neighborhood. "The hidden poor," I started to call them. I was disturbed that so many people in my community had been hidden from my sight before. Once I started making home visits, I realized how desperate many of them were for friends, for people who would care about them without being paid.

Who Is My Poor Neighbor?

There is a wonderful outreach book whose title captures the Christian perspective on poverty – *The Poor Have Faces*. When the church talks about poverty, we are talking about individual people with names and faces, not a soulless group of people that statistics can capture. The people we touch have been uniquely created by God in His image. They are young and old; they live in low-income housing, in shelters, in apartments, in cars in almost every neighborhood in America. They are our neighbors.

Recognizing Our Neighbors

A middle-class man named Mike began to see that his poor neighbors had names and faces. This transformation, from "the homeless" to two particular homeless men with feelings, needs, and personalities, happened over time in a fast-food restaurant where Mike ate weekly before going to Bible study. He writes:

> One day while I was eating, some homeless people came in and sat in the booth behind me. I was thinking, why does that manager let them eat here? The next week I walked in, and there weren't any homeless people. Then the door opened and there they were. They sat in the booth next to me. In anger, I left, thinking, "They have sat in the same booth both times I have been here!"
>
> The next week I sat in a totally different area of the restaurant. I looked out the window, and here they came. They sat in the booth right in front of me. I even had to look at them this time. I began to eavesdrop on their conversation, but I certainly didn't want to make eye contact.
>
> I began to hear a conversation that seemed pretty normal.
>
> "What did you do today?"
> "I went to the store and looked for cans. What about you?"
> "I went over to the day labor corner and worked at Arlington Stadium. I worked all day for $15.00 and after that they took out money for lunch and gas and fees."
> "I guess I'll go back to the park tonight since it's too late to get in the shelter tonight."
> "Yeah, me, too."
>
> I thought to myself, "Why don't you get a better job?" Then I heard,
> "If my legs ever heal, I'm getting out of here."
> "Yeah, if I could afford the medication, I would too."
> "You still hearing those voices?"
> "Yeah."
> "You off your medication?"
> "Yeah. When I'm on that stuff, all I want to do is sleep, and you know what happens when you sleep."
> "Yeah, you get beat up or robbed."[2]

Mike realized that these men were like him. "What would I do if I were in their shoes?" he started to wonder. The realization that they wanted to get out of their situation was eye-opening. Listening to these conversations challenged some of his beliefs about the poor. In fact, this experience was so stirring for Mike that he eventually started a ministry to reach out to homeless men. He never again looked at "those homeless people" in the same way.

Neighbors on Government Welfare

Statistics do not give us an individual snapshot of the welfare family around the corner or in the inner city. Experiencing poverty, conversations with the poor, exposure through poverty ministries – these things make statistical information three-dimensional and personal. Nevertheless, the following statistics can build a skeleton of what poverty looks like.

There are some 5 million families, including 7 million children, on welfare in America.[3] They depend from day to day, from month to month, on government-issued checks. Welfare families are the most dependent families in America. They rely on government assistance because they are not working, have children, and are "needy" by state standards.[4] Generally, when we describe a welfare family, we are talking about a single mother and her kids. Single moms head more than 87 percent of welfare families.[5]

Consider the story of Opal Caples, a welfare recipient who grew up in Chicago, whose story appeared in the *New York Times Magazine:*

> She graduated from high school and got a job at Wendy's. She waited until she was 22 to marry, then waited a year longer to have children, to be sure the marriage would work. It didn't. Her husband quit his job [several years later] for the flash of a drug hustler's life. He moved in with his pregnant girlfriend and left Caples living on welfare. As for their children – Sierra, 7, Kierra, 5, and Tierra, 4 – "he don't call them, he don't see them, he don't buy them nothing."[6]

Although there is no "typical" welfare family, statistics can paint a rough picture:

- Most welfare families have two children.[7]
- Most welfare mothers are between the ages of 20 and 34.[8]
- Fewer than 10 percent of welfare mothers are over the age of 40.[9]
- Fewer than five percent of welfare mothers are teenagers with babies.[10]
- More than 40 percent of welfare recipients have not graduated from high school.[11]
- Fewer than 20 percent of welfare recipients have any college education.[12]
- Half of all welfare recipients have been on welfare for one or more short stays. The other half have received government cash assistance for more than 10 years, uninterrupted.[13]

Welfare families are found in all of the cultures represented in the United States. Historically, the largest number of welfare families has been white. However, African-American and Hispanic families are disproportionately dependent on welfare according to their percentage of the total population. Current statistics show the ethnic and racial breakdown of welfare families as 37 percent African-American, 35 percent white, and 22 percent Hispanic.[14]

Three-fourths of welfare recipients in America live either in rural areas or in central cities.[15] Of African-American families on welfare, over 70 percent live in central cities. More than 60 percent of Hispanic families on welfare live in such areas. Just over 30 percent of white, non-Hispanic families on welfare are residing in central cities, with the majority in rural areas or suburbs.[16]

Generational Welfare Dependency

Welfare families can be divided into two groups – the generational welfare-dependent and the situational welfare-dependent. Welfare families who raise children who, in turn, become welfare recipients are the generational welfare-dependent. Typically, these families have been on welfare more than they have been off welfare.

Sheila, one of the generational welfare-dependent, was doing the best she could as a single parent to raise her three girls. At the same time, her sister, Laurie, was addicted to cocaine and could not adequately care for her two children. Sheila's other sister, Mary, was also a drug addict with two children. Because Sheila believed in God and in His providence, she took in Laurie's and Mary's children.[17]

Sheila was suddenly raising seven children under 14 years of age. The monthly welfare check she received was for her three girls only. Sheila was trying to be a good mother, sister and aunt, but things were becoming desperate.

Generational welfare dependency is the hardest type of welfare dependency for a family to overcome. For a child on welfare, it means that his mother grew up on welfare, and perhaps his mother's mother and his mother's mother's mother. Some children who have grown up in generational poverty have never known working adults in their families or even in their communities. Many of them have never attended weddings or had positive male role models in their lives. Many teenage pregnancies are among children of generational poverty who have never known anything other than welfare dependency and single parenting.

Generational welfare dependency affects much more than family finances – over time, it creates a poverty of spirit that can affect a person's entire being. Worst of all, social welfare history over the last 30 years reveals that such dependency usually destroys the family unit. In the worst cases, this type of poverty overtakes entire neighborhoods, thrusting whole communities into hopelessness and despair. Inner-city neighborhoods are just one image of what generational welfare dependency looks like. It is also found in isolated rural areas.

Situational Welfare Dependency

Situational welfare-dependent families are those who have moved from a state of financial independence to welfare dependence, generally due to crises. Causes of sudden financial hardship include abandonment, divorce, widowhood, debilitating illness, mental illness, domestic violence, substance abuse, job loss, economic recession, and natural disasters. Such crises can cause a family to lose its house, cars, savings, and health insurance. A family that experiences situational welfare dependency may not know anyone else among its relatives or neighbors who has been on welfare. Situational welfare dependency will become generational welfare dependency unless it is stopped.

Laurie Smith became one of the situational welfare-dependent at age 45.[18] Laurie had been married for over 20 years and had two highschool-aged children when her husband left her for another woman. At the same time, Laurie was caring for her terminally ill mother. In the divorce proceedings, Laurie was able to keep her house, but child support payments were sporadic at best, and Laurie was forced to take a second job at night. This job, at a chicken factory, brought on arthritis.

When she could no longer work two jobs, Laurie had to go on welfare. Her mother died that year, and soon after that, Laurie lost the house to bankruptcy. She was, however, determined to get off welfare.

A year after the divorce, Laurie moved to another state to be near her sisters, leaning on them to get herself back on her feet. She still felt as if she were in shock, but she eventually managed to make her way off welfare.

The Challenge of Welfare Dependency

Welfare-dependent families, especially the generational welfare-dependent, need the hope and help that churches can provide. The truth is that the longer a family has been on welfare, the harder it is to get off. The longer a family has been dependent on government social workers, the more likely they are to lack heart-to-heart, trusted relationships. In the worst cases, the only help a family in need receives comes from a government-employed social worker.

Tommy was completely alone when I met him. The night before, on his birthday, he had been so depressed about his loneliness that he had cried himself to sleep. The next morning, he suddenly awoke to find that his bed was on fire. He escaped, but his house burned to the ground.

Tommy was disabled, homeless, jobless, and a recovering alcoholic. The hardest thing for him to handle was the fact that he did not have anyone to call to help him after the fire. As his social worker, I tried to get him back on his feet, but it was impossible without emotional and spiritual support. In desperation, the social services agency made an unconventional decision – it decided to buy Tommy a "friend," someone who would be there for him 24 hours a day. This "friend" would listen to Tommy on the phone and stop by to visit him every couple of days. This arrangement was helpful until Tommy found out, to his intense disappointment, that his new-found friend was being paid to look after him. Eventually, she changed jobs and moved out of his life.

When I last heard from him, Tommy still was struggling with his addictions and dependency. Numerous social workers and temporary friends had come into his life and gone out again, but he still lacked real relationships with people he could trust.

Like Tommy, those neighbors in greatest need are most likely to be hidden from the view of the church. This is not necessarily because they do not know the Lord. Rather, poverty produces loneliness, shame, and self-defeating behaviors that keep many from seeking help from the church.

There are welfare families in nearly every community in America, whether the church sees them or not. Many of these families need trusted friendships that can help them escape poverty. These friendships, which they may not know how to find, are one of the greatest treasures the church has to offer.

Chapter Two

GOOD NEWS FOR THE POOR: WHAT THE BIBLE SAYS

This poor man cried and the Lord heard him, and saved him out of all his troubles.
Psalm 34:6

The exclusion of the weak and insignificant, the seemingly useless people
from a Christian community may actually mean the exclusion of Christ;
the poor brother Christ is knocking at the door.
Dietrich Bonhoeffer[19]

To all outward appearances, Viera and Marie, roommates at a Christian college, might have come from similar backgrounds, with married parents, moderate family income, and houses with two-car garages. After a few weeks of living together, however, Viera shared with Marie that she had grown up in poverty and on welfare. She told Marie that she and her single mom had escaped welfare with the help of a church.

Viera remarked one day, "When you come from poverty, the church offers hope. The only thing people who grow up in poverty see is what is around them. The church offers hope that you can escape by showing you there is more to life than what you've seen." Marie knew that Christians are called to give good news to the poor, but she had never known anyone like Viera before.[20]

Poverty is a major topic in Scripture. In fact, poverty is mentioned in the Bible more often than money. There are over 400 Bible verses about poverty. Because God is concerned about every person who is poor, those who are truly close to God will mirror that concern.

The Causes of Poverty According to Scripture

How does a child like Viera become poor? Some are quick to point out that behavioral sins cause poverty. This type of thinking sounds much like the disciples' quick judgment when they saw a man who had been blind since birth. "Who sinned, this man or his parents, that he was born blind?" they asked. Jesus replied, "Neither this man nor his parents sinned, but this happened so that the work of God might be displayed in his life." (See John 9:1-3.)

It is easy to judge those who are poor as a way to minimize guilt or concern for them. Individual sin can cause poverty, but this is not always the case. A close look at Scripture gives a full picture of the different reasons families become poor.

Viv Grigg, an urban missionary in the slums of the Philippines, spent four years carrying small white cards on which he had hand-copied every Bible verse on poverty. He found that biblical references to poverty could be divided into three main categories derived from five main root Hebrew words (*ebyon, dal, rush, chaser,* and *ani*). He also saw that God's people are called to respond to all causes of poverty.[21]

First, there is poverty caused by personal calamity or the sins of other individuals (*ebyon* and *dal*). People suffering from this kind of poverty include fatherless children, orphans and widows. Its causes can include natural disaster, widowhood, terminal illness, and a physical or mental disability. Psalm 146:9 expresses God's awareness of and care for the dependent poor: "The Lord watches over the sojourners. He upholds the widow and the fatherless." (RSV) Believers are called to find these poor and become a family to them. Job writes, "I was eyes to the blind and feet to the lame. I was a father to the poor and I searched out the cause of him whom I did not know." (Job 29:15-16, RSV)

Second, there is poverty related to personal sin (*chaser*), experienced by those who are poor through laziness (Proverbs 6:10-11), dishonest gain (Proverbs 28:22), compulsiveness (Proverbs 21:5) or the pursuit of pleasure (Proverbs 21:17). This kind of poverty can cause one to continue to sin. Sinful choices that can result from poverty include drunkenness (Proverbs 31:6-7), drug use, stealing (Proverbs 30:8-9), and sexual immorality. Psalm 34:10 offers hope to those who are needy and considering sinful actions: "Those who seek the Lord lack no good thing." (RSV) Believers are called to preach and to live out the gospel through relationships with these poor, and to disciple them.

Third, there is poverty caused by sins of those in power or conquering nations (*ani* and *rush*). Here, oppression rather than calamities or personal sins causes poverty. This oppression could be unjust layoffs, crime (Amos 2:6-7), unjust accusation of a crime, or unjust laws (Isaiah 10:1-2). Proverbs 31:9 speaks to the need for justice in these circumstances, telling believers, "Open your mouth, judge righteously, maintain the rights of the poor and needy." (RSV) We are called to become advocates of these poor by confronting bad social policies and corporate sins.

Welfare dependency can result from any of the above causes. Consider a family that loses its life savings through a terminal illness; an abused teenager who runs away from home, turns to prostitution for income, and becomes pregnant; or a person who is fired for refusing to do something dishonest. God has made these people in His image, and He loves them equally. All three are needful of Christlike love and help to move them beyond their poverty.

The Special Role of the Family with the Poor

If you woke up tomorrow and were poor, whom would you choose to reach out to you – your mother, a pastor, or a social worker? In a crisis, most of us will run to those people whom we can trust and who will be there for us. These trusted relationships start with our family and extend to friends who are most like family.

Scripture supports our natural inclination to turn to our parents, brothers, sisters, grand-parents, cousins, aunts and uncles when we are in need. Families have a special, God-given responsibility to care for their own in trouble. First Timothy 5:3-4 states that families that want to please God are to care for each other:

> Give proper recognition to those widows who are really in need. But if a widow has children or grandchildren, these should learn first of all to put their religion into practice by caring for their own family and so repaying their parents and grandparents, for this is pleasing to God.

Yet welfare families, especially those experiencing generational poverty, may not have family members who can help them out of poverty. Such families often are struggling with tough issues such as single parenting, drug abuse, and juvenile delinquency. Many of their relatives may be on welfare as well.

Someone must become family to those without supportive families of their own. Mother Teresa once said that the AIDS patients she visited in New York City were the poorest of the poor. Their poverty was worse than any she encountered daily in Calcutta. These patients lacked family and trusted relationships to see them through their crises, and in Mother Teresa's opinion, this emotional isolation was worse than financial poverty. Welfare families must deal with both.

The Special Role of the Church with the Poor

While welfare families have social workers who handle their cases from 9 a.m. to 5 p.m., many do not have someone who is there for them when the sun goes down. The big question is this: Who becomes the supportive family to the poor when the family unit is severely broken or nonexistent?

There is a special calling that God has given His church to reach out to the poor and needy. In the absence of family, the church has the privilege of standing in the gap. First Timothy 5 continues:

> If any woman who is a believer has widows in her family, she should help them and not let the church be burdened with them, so that the church can help those widows who are really in need. (5:16)

Scripture also affirms that when we reach out to one of the "hidden poor," we are reaching out to Christ Himself:

> Then the righteous will answer Him, "Lord, when did we see you hungry and feed you, or thirsty and give you something to drink? When did we see you a stranger and invite you in, or needing clothes and clothe you? When did we see you sick or in prison and go to visit you?" The King will reply, "I tell you the truth, whatever you did for one of the least of these brothers of mine, you did for me."[22] (Matthew 25:37-40)

Churches and Their Members

The church is called to be the family for its members who lack family to assist them. In Acts 6, the early church established the role of deacons specifically for the ministry of relief to those in the body who are in need.

Beverly, a single parent on welfare with five children living at home, is a member of a church in Denver. Her church has been learning how to support her since she started working full-time with the goal of staying off welfare. From time to time, for instance, she needs an emergency baby-sitter. As she explains,

> I did not have an extended family or even an immediate family that was there for me. The church has become that extended family. Today my boys are home with the chicken pox; I was fortunate that I found someone who could stay with them so I could go to work.[23]

Beverly at work

Beverly has allowed her local church the privilege of caring for her own. The believer who is poor provides a way for the church to know God better (Jeremiah 22:16), honor Him (Proverbs 14:31), love Him (I John 3:17), and confront each believer's true condition before God (Philippians 2:5-8). It is difficult to say who is more blessed through giving, Beverly or her church.

Churches with Churches

Scripture also speaks of one church financially helping another church, when one is overwhelmed with need and the other has many resources (see 1 Corinthians 16:1-4 and 2 Corinthians 8:1-9:15). Today, this often means suburban churches helping urban churches.

Mike, a pastor at Calvary Baptist Church in the impoverished neighborhood of Compton, California, was thrilled when suburban churches offered their ongoing support to his church's neighborhood ministry:

> We know that to meet the needs of our neighborhood, we must give a variety of services. We have begun with the children, by providing an after-school mentoring and leadership development program. Because they have shown academic and behavioral improvement, we have gained the attention of the parents and can now reach out to minister to them. Programs like job training, literacy, English classes, low-income housing, day care, drug and alcohol treatment centers, and health care centers are all vital parts of our total ministry vision and goals.
>
> As a small 100-member inner-city church, we could never pull this off alone. It is through partnerships with other ministries, especially suburban churches, that we can accomplish our ambitious outreach plans. We are cur-

rently in some form of partnership with three suburban churches. Coast Hills Community Church has assisted us in providing merchandise for a student-run thrift store whose profits are used for college scholarships for children. They are helping us purchase a building to permanently house the thrift store. Coastland Community Church has brought down its congregation for racial reconciliation gatherings, and has appointed a person to stay in contact with us to determine how it can continue to partner with us in reaching the children and families in Compton. And Calvary Church [of Santa Ana] came down and repaved our entire parking lot free of charge.[24]

Churches and Non-Members

In Deuteronomy 10:18, we see that God's concern for the needy extends beyond the body of believers. God's treatment of the "stranger" in this passage expresses His love for those outside the church who are in need: "He administers justice for the fatherless and the widow, and loves the stranger, giving him food and clothing." (KJV)

Our ministry to those outside the church, who do not know Jesus Christ, is one of the chief ways we bring glory to God. The gospel – literally, the "good news" – is displayed through our actions. Jesus proclaimed in Matthew 5:14a, 16, "You are the light of the world. ...Let your light shine before men, that they may see your good deeds and praise your Father in heaven."

Viera, when she was a child on welfare, was not a member of a church. She describes how she received the "good news":

> When I was twelve, a single man in a local church decided to make the kids in my neighborhood his ministry. Every week, he picked some of us up and took us to youth group on Wednesday night. I was hesitant to go to church at first, because I didn't want to wear a dress, and I didn't know anyone there. When I finally went, the girls in the group wanted to be my friend. No one treated me as if I was different. I decided to go back every week.
>
> We always lived in small, trashy apartments with rats and holes in the walls. Money was always a problem. When the leaders in the youth group discovered I was poor, they offered to pay for me to attend the activities and retreats the youth group went on. Five months after I started attending church, I went on my first youth group retreat, and it changed my life. After hearing one of the speakers, I asked Jesus to be my Savior.[25]

Viera's story emphasizes the hope the church can provide for those outside its walls. Through the church's love, she found the love of Jesus Christ. And through the church's vision for her long-term welfare, Viera's family was able to rise above poverty:

> A woman in the church observed my desire to grow spiritually. She knew that the school system in my neighborhood was bad and I would not benefit academically or spiritually. She saw potential in me and wanted me to be in an environment that would give me a strong future. With this in mind, she went before our church board and asked them to admit me into the

Christian school. Not only was I accepted, but the church also worked out an arrangement with my family and other families in the church to help cover the costs of a private school.

When I started going to the Christian school, my mom saw that I was getting an education, so she wanted to better herself. She wanted to get off welfare, so she got a job at a factory. She realized that welfare would never allow her to take care of her family.[26]

It is a privilege for God's people to reach out to welfare families, some of the poorest of the poor in the United States. This is one way we bring "good news" to these hidden poor for the greater glory of our Savior.

Chapter Three

A HAND UP FROM POVERTY: WHAT WELFARE REFORM MEANS

But seek the welfare of the city … and pray to the Lord on its behalf,
for in its welfare you will find your welfare.
Jeremiah 29:7b (RSV)

If every church and synagogue in the United States took in 10 families
who are on welfare, we would eliminate welfare.
Reverend Billy Graham[27]

Jan Tuls, a 53-year-old wife and grandmother in Michigan, never expected to gain notoriety through her friendship with Maria Gonzalez. Maria, 27, was a recent divorcee and mother of four. She recently had become homeless and was making the transition from welfare to work when they met. Maria needed emotional support to be successful in her new, second-shift job inspecting car windows. She also needed practical support with such issues as day care for her children and transportation to her job.

When Jan's church, Calvary Christian Reformed Church, "adopted" Maria, a welfare client of Ottawa County social services (known as the Family Independence Agency), Jan became her mentor. Due to Maria's successful transition from welfare to work, her friendship with Jan had national implications. *USA Today* stated, "Maria Gonzalez thanks God for her move from welfare to work." Of her friendship with Jan, Maria told *USA Today*, "She's more of a mom to me than my own."[28]

The Disappearance of Welfare as We Knew It

In the wake of welfare reform, the behind-the-scenes work of Jan Tuls and Calvary Christian Reformed Church is front and center in the reshaping of charity in America. Due to a major change in the law, each parent on welfare is facing today one of the great challenges of his or her life. It is no longer an option to stay on welfare – a family like Maria's must leave welfare for good.

In 1996, America changed 60 years of social welfare policy. "Welfare as we knew it" ended under a federal law called the Personal Responsibility and Work Opportunity Reconciliation Act (PRWORA).[29] The federal program called Aid to Families with Dependent Children (AFDC) was replaced with an entirely new federal block grant program called Temporary Assistance to Needy Families (TANF).[30]

TANF requires that welfare-dependent families, including the generational welfare-dependent, get off welfare and stay off forever. This is true even for welfare moms who have little or no job experience, live in the inner city, have sick children, are overcome with chronic depression, or have a substance abuse problem.[31] Most families are only eligible for welfare cash assistance for five years over their entire lives. Before the change in the law, welfare families could receive benefits over their entire lives, once they qualified. (See the appendix for more information.)

The Creation of a Social Disaster

Franklin D. Roosevelt concurred at the start of the AFDC program that it best served families as a short-term solution and would be a social disaster if families stayed on it too long:

> The lessons of history, confirmed by the evidence immediately before me, show conclusively that continued dependence upon relief induces a spiritual and moral disintegration fundamentally destructive to national fiber. To dole out relief in this way is to administer a narcotic, a subtle destroyer of human spirit. It is inimical to the dictates of sound policy. It is a violation of the traditions of America.[32]

What Welfare Caused

Giving welfare families a hand up from poverty is not a simple task. The old AFDC program had many unintended, long-term consequences for our neighbors on welfare. (See the appendix for more information.)

Overcoming welfare dependency first means acknowledging that thousands of welfare families have lost all hope that they can ever escape it. As one woman put it, "I feel … trapped by it. I have been on it for about 12 years, too. My daughter is 12 and I think that you just get caught up in the cycle of it. You just can't get out of it."[33] The longer a family has been on welfare, the harder it is to get off. Leaving welfare means overcoming a dependent state of mind and spirit and years of adapted behavior. The former welfare recipient must overcome material poverty, familial poverty, behavioral poverty, spiritual poverty, and emotional poverty, often "swimming against the tide" of community mores that support a culture of dependency.

Overcoming welfare dependency also requires the realization that the institutions that can best serve the poor have been severely affected by welfare policy. Welfare as we knew it indirectly helped to destroy the family unit, the first measure of protection for the poorest of the poor. Over 19 million American children are growing up today in fatherless families, whereas in 1960, 5 million children lived in female-headed households.[34] When President Lyndon B. Johnson's War on Poverty began in 1964, the out-of-wedlock birth rate was one-quarter what it is today.[35] Even the extended family has been severely affected by long-term welfare dependency.

In addition, welfare as we knew it indirectly affected the church, the second measure of protection for the poor. Benevolence giving has been on the decline since the increase in government welfare programs.[36] At the turn of the 20th century, society viewed the church as an urban institution. To speak of the city was to speak of the domain of the church. Today, church resources are weakest where the needs of the poor are greatest, with the majority of church spending going to suburban church growth.[37] Some churches have succumbed to a culture of comfort rather than one of sacrifice.

A Time of Rapid Change

The welfare reform legislation began a time of upheaval for everyone concerned with welfare families. One expert told a congressional committee, "In thirty years of observing welfare policy making and administration, I have never seen a period of such rapid change."[38] The goal of welfare reform is to uplift the poor by helping them become economically self-sufficient. Everyone involved wants welfare families to come through this transition successfully. No one wants to see them suffer.

For their part, welfare recipients must change their self-concept from dependent to independent. They are now responsible to obtain jobs, some for the first time in their lives, in order to provide for their families. They must find child care, transportation, and emotional support to be successful in their jobs – and they have a short window of time in which to do this.

On July 1, 1997, all states set in motion their plans to move their welfare families off welfare.[39] With a five-year maximum lifetime benefit, the first group of welfare families will be required to leave public assistance forever in the year 2002. Each year thereafter, thousands of welfare families will no longer be eligible for welfare assistance.[40] The generational welfare-dependent face the greatest challenges in this time of change. Many are considered among the "hardest to employ." They need ongoing emotional support and intensive, holistic help to overcome the barriers preventing them from holding a job (e.g., addictions or domestic violence recovery). Their move from welfare to work won't happen overnight.

All 50 states must change their approach to their welfare-dependent families. The welfare law makes each state legally responsible for developing and implementing a plan to move its welfare families into jobs and off government assistance. Social service departments, for their part, are changing from a cash assistance approach to a job placement approach. Many other government departments are changing to ensure that they get their welfare families to work in the next few years. Each state is experimenting with various approaches during this transition. The hope is that, with 50 different experiments taking place, the best methods to help these poor become financially independent will emerge.

The faith community must change its outreach practices in light of welfare reform. Many churches are turning their handout ministries into hand-up ministries. State and local governments are encouraging the creation of church-based mentoring and employment ministries for welfare families. They see churches as crucial in building one-on-one supportive relationships with the toughest-to-employ welfare recipients. Many are developing formal and informal partnerships with churches to move families off welfare.[41] Also, the welfare reform legislation includes funding opportunities for churches that are assisting welfare recipients into jobs by providing such services as child care. Churches and faith-based nonprofits can contract or receive vouchers from their local governments without having to alter their religious character. (See the appendix on the rules under Section 104, called the *Charitable Choice Provision*.)

The Church Is Coming

For the first time in more than 60 years, federal, state, and local governments are doing whatever they can to ensure that "the church is coming" to help families off welfare. Why? Many know that government-only approaches to lift welfare families out of poverty have had limited success. When the welfare reform law of 1996 passed, the president, governors, and county commissioners made it clear that welfare reform's success depended partly on the degree to which the church helped welfare families get jobs and keep jobs. Then-Governor Kirk Fordice of Mississippi went so far as to say, "God, not government, will be the savior of welfare recipients."[42]

No other group can take the church's place in welfare reform. Bill Raymond, a Christian social worker in Michigan, explains, "The church should do [now] what it can do best – and what the government can't do at all: engage in transformational relationships."[43]

This is a watershed moment for churches. Many states and counties are asking their churches to become a supportive family for welfare families. Sacramento County Welfare Director Cheryl Davis, from a county that must help more than 40,000 welfare families make the transition to work, said, "Our office can't handle those [sic] kind of numbers, so it's great the churches are coming in. From the beginning, we saw faith-based communities as an important part of welfare reform."[44] Ottawa County (Mich.) Welfare Director Loren Snippe, who has 260 churches in his jurisdiction, compares this ministry opportunity to that presented by the Vietnam War: "After the Vietnam War, many churches sponsored families from Southeast Asia. We asked them why they can't do that with families around the corner."[45]

The Challenge before the Church

Welfare reform presents a great challenge to our churches. In fact, how the church responds to welfare reform will shape the future of our country. The church's response to local welfare families will influence their beliefs about the church. Welfare families will not hope in the church unless the church gives them reason to hope by loving them through this critical transition. For churches, this starts with recognizing the critical needs of welfare families, needs the government cannot adequately fill.

Welfare moms and dads need jobs. They need reliable and affordable transportation to their jobs, which often are located outside their neighborhoods. They need affordable and accessible child care consistent with their family beliefs. Most of all, they need ongoing, supportive relationships to help them over the many hurdles associated with going to work and other significant changes.

The church's response to welfare reform will be a factor in the to-be-determined success of the welfare reform legislation of 1996.[46] Former Governor David Beasley of South Carolina captured the monumental implications of welfare reform's success or failure:

> If it succeeds, we can all take pride in the lives that were changed. But if families are allowed to fall further into poverty, we're going to see an outcry for a network of social programs wider and deeper than before. In this transition, every job is crucial. Every family is valued. Every government leader, every industry leader, every loving neighbor has a vital part to play.[47]

The church's response to welfare families will also shape the government's response to the church. If churches are successful in restoring hope and dignity to welfare families, the government will be more likely to embrace faith-based initiatives in the future. This will impress upon the country the important role of the faith community in restoring our communities and could open the door for further legislation to make it easier for faith-based providers and churches to provide services to the poorest of the poor.

Finally, the church's response to welfare families will shape the future of Christian charity. If churches see themselves on the front lines of charity, rather than in the background, they will commit more time and resources to the needs in our communities. Church outreach will begin to change as well, as more churches address root problems rather than providing temporary relief for the poor. Most importantly, America's churches will be revived through loving our neighbors, particularly our neighbors in great need.

Churches Can Lead the Way

The suburban community of Ottawa County, Michigan, where Jan Tuls and Maria Gonzales live, provides an example of the impact churches can have on the country by loving families off welfare. In October 1997, this county of 220,000 people and 260 churches received nationwide attention for being the first county in the country to employ every able-bodied welfare recipient. This accomplishment was a direct result of the work of average churchgoers, such as Jan Tuls, who provided ongoing, relational and practical support to welfare recipients in their cities.[48]

The *Washington Post* trumpeted Ottawa County's success on its front page, giving special attention to the work of these ordinary churchgoers:

Neighbors took [a welfare mother's] children shopping for school clothes. Executives for a local manufacturer helped her find work. Bob and Mary Ann Baker bought her a used car to get around. Ginny Weerstra [her mentor from Hardewyk Reformed Christian Church] helped her find an apartment. Parishioners at Hardewyk Reformed Christian Church took up a collection to get her phone installed, and when her husband reentered her life, Pastor Andrew Gorter provided the couple with marital counseling.[49]

What happened in Ottawa County can happen in every city and county in America. It starts with churches such as Hardewyk Reformed Christian Church doing the things they do best – preaching the gospel, loving their neighbors, and giving a hand up to the needy.

Chapter Four

A VISION FOR OUTREACH: OUR CHURCHES AND THE POOR

Your people will rebuild the ancient ruins
And will raise up the age-old foundations;
You will be called Repairer of Broken Walls,
Restorer of Streets with Dwellings.
Isaiah 58:12

A church must seek an impact on nothing less than the
entire community and its social system.[50]
Timothy Keller, senior pastor, Redeemer Presbyterian Church, New York City

Tom, a Nazarene pastor, felt a calling to rebuild a run-down section of his city. After much prayer, his church adopted a neighborhood where a volunteer group started spending regular time. In time, the church purchased an abandoned, condemned building to turn into a housing unit for the community's homeless.

Pastor Tom met Rita the day the building's sale closed. He was walking through the dark, cold building, imagining the hope it would provide the community, when he encountered a woman in a hallway. She was shocked to be face to face with a pastor inside the condemned building. She was even more surprised when Pastor Tom told her a church was coming.

Tom could not believe what this mother of two told him. Rita was a single parent, welfare-dependent, without trusted family support, and feeling hopeless. Her family had been secretly living in the condemned building without heat or hot water for years. They had just endured one of the bitter cold Washington, D.C., winters.[51] As he listened to her story, Tom began to wonder: What does a church do when it comes face to face with a woman like Rita?

Is Our Vision Limited?

Churches take various approaches to welfare mothers. One church would refer Rita to the local department of social services, another would refer her to a secular nonprofit, and still another would refer her to another church. Many churches would pray with Rita; most would share the gospel with her. Some would give her money or canned goods, and others would engage concerned laity in helping her more personally. There are also churches that would tell Rita they couldn't assist her.

It is hard for many to imagine what church-based ministry to Rita, a woman on welfare, looks like. Since the time of our great-grandparents, impoverished families have depended on both the church and the government to meet their needs. Some churches have found themselves shaping their own roles with families in need in response to the government's role. When the government has been on the front lines, these churches have played a lesser role. When the government has been on the sidelines, these churches have expanded their outreach efforts.

Over the last 100 years, Americans have witnessed four key periods of government involvement in helping families in poverty: the pre-Depression period (prior to 1925), the Depression to the Great Society period (1925-1964), the Great Society period (1965-1995), and the welfare reform period (1996 to the present). Out of each period, a model for church outreach to the poor has evolved – each model with its own strengths and weaknesses in ministering to welfare families. Today, as many churches still continue to follow these patterns, it is challenging to find a common vision for church-based outreach to the poor, including welfare families.

Each of these models is named after a biblical character whose struggles it reflects. Each has arisen unintentionally on the part of churches. Each has come about as a response to the government's involvement, or lack of involvement, with those in need. And each incorporates the secular thinking of the time period from which it arose into a vision, usually unvoiced, about the church's role with the poor.

The "Samson Church" – Acting Alone

The "Samson church" sees the church's strengths in outreach to the poor. Like the biblical character Samson, these churches view themselves as strong and capable of handling just about anything. They are well aware that the church has been involved in massive outreach efforts in America's history and that prior to the Great Depression churches were leading the way in outreach. In fact, their view of the church's role is based largely on America's pre-Depression view of the church. Today, some "Samson churches" are so optimistic about the church's capacity for ministering to "the hidden poor" that they would prefer to see government programs for the poor removed overnight.

The chief strength of the "Samson church" is that its vision for outreach puts the church on the front lines of outreach efforts in the community. Church members believe that they should be able to minister to anyone, anywhere, anytime. Their desire is to meet proactively the needs around them and not to refer a family in need to another group. If a needed ministry doesn't exist, they will strive to create it. They are the least likely to collaborate with other Christian groups or social services – a fact that actually leads to their greatest weakness.

The insulated approach of a "Samson church" toward ministering among the poor does not move it to co-labor with other churches or social services toward shared goals. Members of these churches also lack understanding of how government programs and community structures affect the poor in their city. These churches generally have large outreach budgets and strive to maintain ownership of their ministries, rather than "coming alongside" the work of others. More often than not, the poor they seek to help live outside the neighborhood of the church and may not feel comfortable with the church's middle-class subculture.

A "Samson church" might say to a woman on welfare, "We will help you get out of poverty. If we don't have a way to help you, we will create a way to help you. If we don't have the resources to help you, we will find the money to help you. But, somehow, let us help you."

The "Moses Church" – Not Responsible

The "Moses church" sees the church's weaknesses in outreach to the poor. Like the biblical character Moses when called by God to lead the people out of Egypt, members of this kind of church don't feel adequate for the task in front of them. These churches reflect the mindset of the Depression era, when the government stepped in to assist with the great needs during the employment crisis of the '30s. Churches during that period saw the government reduce its role at the beginning of World War II and grew comfortable with the government's maintenance role with the poor in the '50s and early '60s. This was also a period of great growth for parachurch ministries, many of which developed to fill an outreach void left by churches.

Today, most "Moses churches" are ambivalent about the church's capacity for ministering to "the hidden poor" and expect some maintenance of effort from government programs. They count on the fact that there are other community agencies to help the poor and that if there were a crisis, the government would step in. They have also witnessed the growth of government programs as opposed to faith-based programs and have forgotten that churches were once the first place the poor went for assistance. Most churches in America have adopted the "Moses" model.

The chief strength of the "Moses church" is that it is comfortable referring the poor to other groups for assistance. This church has identified a few community ministries to which it can refer people and has something of a structure in place to assist with short-term needs. It is comfortable letting other groups assist with deep needs, much as Moses was comfortable with God using Aaron in his stead. Many of them, for instance, prefer merely to play the role of a "third party" with the poor by giving money to a parachurch organization or to their denominations to help those in need.

Yet the "Moses church" is perhaps the most dangerous of all the outreach models because it doesn't have a focused outreach vision. These churches are ambivalent about the church's ability to meet the greatest needs of the community. They believe that the church has a role in meeting physical and emotional human needs, but, in practice, they don't reach out to those in need. "Moses churches" are primarily involved in relief efforts such as church-run clothes closets or food banks to help the needy, rather than addressing the root causes of poverty. Also, they do not intentionally strive to build long-term relationships with those in need in their community.

A "Moses church" might say to a woman on welfare, "We want to help you through your crisis. Go to this other church and see if they can help you with your long-term needs. Here are the hours of our church-run food pantry. Let us pray for you before you go."

The "Sarah Church" – Misplaced Faith

The "Sarah church" sees the government's strengths in outreach to the poor. Just as the biblical character Sarah gave up hope that she could become pregnant and asked Hagar to be her contingency plan, "Sarah churches" have lost hope in the church and are utilizing other systems to meet the needs around them.

These churches remember the "Great Society" period, from the '60s through the early '90s, when government assumed a primary role in helping the needy. Unlike the "Moses church," these churches are not ambivalent about their role; they are quite definite in their belief that their role is secondary to that of the government.

Today, many laypeople in "Sarah churches" are serving the poor through government programs, and from that vantage point, they have become cynical about the church's capacity for helping the poor. Many of them have actually witnessed the retreat of the Christian community's outreach to the poorest of the poor. They would rather see more government programs to assist the needy because they trust more in these systems than in the church. Many "Sarah churches" preach a message of deliverance for the poor that depends on greater government involvement to meet the deepest needs.

The chief strength of the "Sarah church" is the expertise within its laity regarding government systems and programs. They understand how to connect the poor with government resources and are keenly aware when these services do not alleviate human need. They are also highly mobilized to hold the government accountable for how it assists the poor.

The greatest weakness of the "Sarah church" is its willingness to depend on government assistance that fails to address the spiritual needs of the poor. Members of such churches have lost a vision for outreach that is holistic, whose message of hope rests in the person of Jesus Christ. Their vision is primarily focused on deliverance from physical need by government programs.

The "Sarah church" might say to a woman on welfare, "Our church can connect you with a social worker who can provide more resources for your situation. Everyone deserves to stay on welfare as long as possible in this time of transition. We will do our best to make sure you don't lose your welfare benefits."

The "Esther Church" – Courting Government

The "Esther church" sees both the church's and the government's strengths in outreach to the poor. Like the biblical character Esther, these churches will work within the government system to accomplish their Christ-centered goals of assisting those who need help. These churches are motivated by the needs presented by the welfare reform legislation of 1996 as well as the funding opportunities available for churches through this legislation. "Esther churches" have renewed hope in the church and are excited to work with like-minded government officials toward shared goals.

Right now these churches see a huge task in front of them in lifting families, particularly welfare families, out of poverty. Many will accept government funding if it helps advance their church's ministries in meeting these needs. They believe the poor can be helped through the church and that the church's outreach to the poor will look different from the way it looked in times past. They are comfortable relying on government-based instruction on how they can assist the "least of these" during this time of transition for welfare families.

The greatest strength of the "Esther church" is its focus on advancing its outreach ministries for welfare families. "Esther churches" are educated on the welfare reform legislation, particularly the Charitable Choice Provision (see the appendix). They are eager to do something to help welfare families find independence.

The greatest weakness of the "Esther church" is its responsive posture to government. Its vision is informed by short-lived changes in the law rather than the permanent truths of the Bible. Because of this, such churches can easily subscribe to the secular vision presented in welfare reform, that of merely moving welfare families into jobs, rather than playing a prophetic and evangelistic role with the poor and with the government systems that are designed to serve them. They fail to see that the church has an opportunity to present a higher vision for outreach that promises to inspire even government officials.

The "Esther church" might say to a woman on welfare, "We will help you off welfare. Let us call your social worker to find out what we can do for you. In the interim, we will help you with your short-term needs."

A Higher Calling – A Biblical Model

The church needs a vision for outreach to the poor that transcends the world's vision. "Samson," "Moses," "Sarah," and "Esther" churches are in danger of belying their mission. If the church does not see a role for the government in assisting the needy, it is not giving voice to government's legitimate role with those who cannot care for themselves – the elderly, the permanently disabled, abused and neglected children, and so on. Likewise, if the church is responding to government policies first, whether intentionally or unintentionally, it is putting government in the place of God. The church's vision will be limited to a utilitarian function. It will also have the ring of idolatry, as the master served will cease to be the Lord Himself.[52]   The church's vision must go beyond the secular sphere.

If the church's vision for outreach rests on the equipping that God alone can provide through His Word and His Spirit, every church will be able to shine its light in such a way that the poor will know that they can come in any season, in any political climate, for hope, love, and help out of their impoverished situation. This God-given vision will bring the church and the poor face to face with Jesus and inspire all, including the government, with that true light that shines brightest in the darkness.

A Vision for Outreach

Ministry among current and former welfare families should be a part of each church's larger outreach vision. Isaiah 61:1-3 is a good place to start to find a biblical vision for church-based outreach to the poor:

> The Spirit of the Sovereign Lord is on me, because the Lord has anointed me to preach good news to the poor. He has sent me to bind up the brokenhearted, to proclaim freedom for the captives and release from darkness for the prisoners, to proclaim the year of the Lord's favor and the day of vengeance of our God, to comfort all who mourn, and provide for those who grieve in Zion – to bestow on them a crown of beauty instead of ashes, the

oil of gladness instead of mourning, and a garment of praise instead of a spirit of despair. They will be called oaks of righteousness, a planting of the Lord for the display of His splendor.

Consider what this passage says to your church when it comes face to face with a family on welfare, outside the church, isolated from supportive relationships, and feeling hopeless.[53]

Preach Good News to the Poor

Every church has been anointed to preach good news to the poor. Sharing the good news of Jesus Christ is an integral part of the church's outreach vision for the needy. A church with this vision would speak to a welfare family of the good news found in Jesus Christ. It would also mirror the faith of the Christian family on welfare that has dutifully trusted God and prayed for deliverance from government dependence.

Restore the Poor to Wholeness

Each church has the privilege of restoring the poor to wholeness. This is a holistic calling that moves the church to aid, comfort and provide for the poor. If a welfare mother has the God-given desire to be restored to wholeness, the church begins to be a blessing to her on a holistic level. This reciprocal relationship starts with addressing the deep needs in her life — including her financial needs, her parenting needs, and her relational needs.

Restoring the poor to wholeness inspires a church to move beyond relief efforts to development efforts in its outreach ministries. This is where root causes and community-wide systemic issues are brought to light, where community collaboratives begin, and where individual discipleship occurs. This is the point where a church begins to help move a welfare mother off welfare so she, too, can share in God's calling to be a blessing to her family and be freed from her captivity.

Transformation of the Poor

Every church can be a participant in the transformation of the poor, so much so that the poor will one day be called "oaks of righteousness, a planting of the Lord for the display of His splendor." (Isaiah 61:3b) Every church, with God's love and grace, can be a part of a welfare mother's complete transformation – a transformation that is holistic (spiritual, emotional, physical, mental, and social). This transformation goes beyond what money or hard work can accomplish.

God's desire is to display His glory through the lives of people like Rita, the welfare mother in the abandoned building. When a church comes face to face with a woman like Rita, God's reach is not so short that she, too, could not be called an "oak of righteousness" someday.

God's Big Vision

God's vision for the poor does not stop with the transformation of the poor. If we read further in Isaiah 61:4, we find an even higher call for the church's outreach ministries:

They will rebuild the ancient ruins and restore the places long devastated; they will renew the ruined cities that have been devastated for generations.

The "good news" is that the word *they* in this passage refers to the poor, even the welfare mother. The poor the church restores, with God's help, become the homegrown leaders that God often uses to restore an entire block, a neighborhood, or even a city. The goal of church-based outreach, as the Christian Community Development Association aptly puts it, is "to develop people to the point where they are using their God-given skills and abilities in satisfying work that is also benefiting the community."[54]

Ministry to welfare recipients allows each church to participate in God's "big" vision for community transformation. As the end of her story shows, Rita's personal transformation, brought about by the church, brought God's blessing not only on her own family, but on her entire community as well.

God's Vision in Action

After Pastor Tom's church came to Rita's building, she started going to Sunday services, though she was still hesitant about what the church might do. As a child in poverty, she had been turned off to churches at an early age. Rita remembered hearing her great-grandmother speak about Jesus helping whenever there was a need. At age 11, therefore, she had gone to a church to find Jesus. But Rita's family of 10 could not afford the proper clothes to wear, and one Sunday she heard women in the church talking about her arriving in the same outfit every week. She ran away from the church, promising herself that she would go back only after she owned the nicest clothes.

Rita's view of the church started to change after Pastor Tom arrived. Teenagers arrived one summer from all over, even from as far away as Kansas, to help restore her abandoned, condemned building. The church even dedicated the offering collection to renovate the building and to provide health services and educational enrichment for people in the community.

Everything came to a head for Rita when one day, in her renovated apartment, she started crying. All the times she had been hungry, homeless, and lost when she was a little girl suddenly came back to her, but now she heard Christ saying that He had been there all the time.

Pastor Tom's church was committed to helping Rita off welfare. Rita began by volunteering at the church's community health center in order to learn job skills. She became the receptionist for the main doctor. Not knowing how to answer the telephone and wanting to do the best job she could, Rita called area hospitals to see how other receptionists would answer. In time, she became office manager. Rita successfully worked her way off welfare within a year.

Rita has been a part of Pastor Tom's church since 1977 and is an inspiration to all who know her. She is now known to her neighbors as the neighborhood outreach leader and community organizer. She has given hope and practical help to hundreds of families coming off welfare. Among other things, she has started a neighborhood-owned Laundromat called *BIG WASH* (Believers in God Working at Spiritual Healing), a job readiness program called Entrée, and a drug prevention program called *Let's Make a Deal*. Her story and good works have been featured in several publications and books, including *People* magazine and *The Washington Post.*

Rita literally has saved many lives in her neighborhood. Her story is a testimony to the new life that the church can give a welfare family. She shows that one changed life can affect a home, a street, a neighborhood, a city, and a country for the hidden poor.[55]

Chapter Five

NEW LIFE FOR THE POOR: ONE CHURCH'S STORY

Religion that God our Father accepts as pure and faultless is this:
to look after orphans and widows in their distress.
James 1:27a

The revived church by many or by few is moved to engage in evangelism,
in teaching and in social action.
James Edwin Orr[56]

One church in Denver, Heritage Christian Center, vowed to open its doors as wide as possible to the poor. The church was born from an 11-person Bible study that met in the pastor's basement and prayed, "Lord, send us everybody in this city that nobody else wants." Their goals were to love people, win souls, see people set free, and encourage the body of Christ in missionary outreach throughout the world. In 1985, the church adopted the mission statement: "Touching a Hurting World with the Love of Jesus Christ." Less than 10 years later, they were an 11,000-member church composed of low-income and middle-class families.

God used two people to infect the church with His vision for outreach. Senior Pastor Dennis Leonard had a unique and life-changing vision to pull down racial barriers and become a church for all people. As Pastor Leonard began to move toward this goal, the overwhelming agony of the poor, both those who were working and those on welfare, gripped his heart. The prejudice of the ages and the destruction of the family became a call to action. Associate Pastor Debbie Stafford, a former welfare recipient, knew the desperation of families in need, especially welfare families. (See Preface for her story.) She gave her personal insight to the church as it developed many outreach programs and practical ministries.

From Short-Term Relief to Long-Term Development

The outreach ministries of the church began by relieving short-term crises: feeding the

The congregation of Heritage Christian Center

homeless, providing temporary assistance to unwed mothers, giving emergency assistance, and praying for those in need. As word spread throughout the community, calls for assistance climbed to over 100 per day. In order to meet the needs of the people, Pastor Leonard hired the church's first outreach pastor, Pastor Dave McFann.

Soon, the church began to expand its existing ministries beyond relief work to address the long-term developmental needs in its community. This meant, in part, starting various support groups, including one for recovering drug addicts and another for abused women. The church was developing systems to reach out to the greatest needs in its community, especially those needs that weren't already being met by other churches and ministries.

Under Pastor Dave, the church developed a ministry with long-term impact: a shelter to move families out of homelessness. Due to government regulations, shelter services were suspended in 1996, because the church was not allowed to house a Christian school and a shelter within close proximity of one another. Although this was a temporary set-back, the church was not deterred in its outreach vision.

Intentional Relationships with the Needy

In 1996, the year the monumental welfare legislation was signed into law, the church developed a ministry to meet the needs of transitioning welfare families, building on the goals of the former shelter. This new ministry, called Project Heritage, is providing transitional housing for adults on welfare and their children, and on-the-job employment training, both at a former Air Force base. It is currently developing a child-care center there, as well. Project Heritage is pointing the way for the church to find the "hidden people" in its community and help even the hardest to employ obtain jobs and find new hope for their lives.

Betsy, for example, was imprisoned in a state penitentiary for nine years for committing a felony.[57] When she came to Heritage Christian Center, she did not relate to people very well, she was angry, and she had minimal job skills. Initially, Heritage Christian Center provided her with food, clothing, and bus tokens necessary to obtain a job. Through the efforts of Project Heritage, she got a night janitorial job at a recreational center in a suburb outside Denver. As she was filled with hope for her life, she attended ministry courses the church offered. She is now a principal volunteer in the church's prison ministry, helping others get their lives turned around.

Project Heritage also helped Nancy, a woman who was charged with a felony.[58] Though she was not sentenced to a prison term, the felony charge cost Nancy everything. In order to support herself and her children, she became a prostitute in Denver. When she came to the church, she was homeless, destitute, and emotionally broken. Project Heritage helped her with housing, transportation, food, and pastoral counseling. As her life stabilized and she regained hope in God, Nancy became a volunteer with the church's community outreach ministries, helping people find housing resources. She is now the Housing Coordinator at Project Heritage.

Janet, a single welfare mother, had only a few months to make the transition from welfare to work when she came to Project Heritage.[59] Due to the church's relationship with the county department of social services, Janet found out about Project Heritage and believed that it would give her the skills necessary to move to full-time employment. The stakes for Janet were high. She was banking the well-being of her 10-year-old twins – one of whom is on medication for Attention Deficit Disorder and requires much one-on-one attention – that this church would get her into a job before her welfare benefits ran out.

Project Heritage brings hope to the community

How a Church Began a Ministry to Welfare Families

Project Heritage was born in 1996 when a mission-minded congregation decided to put feet to its mission statement, "Touching a Hurting World with the Love of Jesus Christ."

1   The outreach pastor of the church, Dave McFann, started a homeless shelter at the church. When the homeless shelter was forced to close due to zoning conflicts, his vision grew. He formulated the concept for Project Heritage, a ministry that would establish the church within the community, allowing it to meet more needs and receive greater community support.

2   Pastor McFann gained support for this new ministry idea from the church. He knew launching a ministry of this magnitude would take two to three years, and that it would be impossible without the emotional, physical, spiritual, and financial support of the church.

3   Heritage Christian Center hired an attorney from a sympathetic law firm to do the legal filing to create a separate nonprofit. Project Heritage was legally born when it became a 501(c)(3) nonprofit, legally separate from Heritage Christian Center but under its home missions umbrella.

4   A real estate agent from the congregation began to look for buildings near the church that it could purchase and renovate. Once a site was located, it took the church almost two years to work through the obstacles of rezoning and gaining support from neighborhood groups. This was a

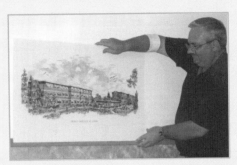

Pastor Dave McFann
Project Heritage

real strain on the church, and there were times when the members thought of giving up on the project.

5 Project Heritage decided to purchase two residential properties located on the former Lowry Air Force Base. The project obtained a loan from the local bank to pay the $618,000 acquisition fee. Heritage Christian Center co-signed the loan.

6 Project Heritage needed to raise $4.1 million dollars for the renovation of the two properties. It initially approached the Department of Housing and Urban Development (HUD) for assistance. Working with HUD involved so many restrictions, however, that the project members gave up on that idea, realizing that it would force them to dilute their program and lose sight of their vision. Project Heritage next approached several local bankers. A local bank made a commitment to provide a 30-year, $3 million renovation loan.

7 In the beginning, Heritage Christian Center "loaned" one part-time and three full-time staff members to Project Heritage. After the first year, these "loaned" staff members went on the payroll of Project Heritage, as required by the laws governing nonprofits. Project Heritage still continues to receive great volunteer support from Heritage Christian Center.

8 In year one, Heritage Christian Center provided 100 percent of the funding for Project Heritage. In the second year, Project Heritage raised funds from businesses, foundations, private donors, and local government grants. That same year, Heritage Christian Center reduced its financial support to two-thirds of Project Heritage's budget. While the ministry depended initially on the church's financial support, its long-term financial goal is to be self-supporting.

9 Project Heritage is meeting the final criteria before renovating its 63 zoned apartments and on-site child care center. Renovations are currently underway. Once renovations are complete, about 200 individuals at a time will be able to receive transitional housing. Project Heritage will then be able to help transform the lives of the poor in its community through its own short-term housing as well as its job training, job placement, child care, and counseling programs.

10 Already, Project Heritage has served over 750 welfare families and has helped approximately 150 of these families into jobs. While the residential side of Project Heritage is being completed, it is referring families in need to temporary housing and providing funding for them. The project is also working on buying a hotel to meet the short-term housing needs of these families.

For more information, contact:
Project Heritage • 9495 East Florida Avenue • Denver, CO 80231 • Phone: (303) 873-1514
Fax: (303) 337-2051
or
Heritage Christian Center • 9495 East Florida Avenue • Denver, CO 80231 • Phone: (303) 369-8514
Fax: (303) 337-2051 • Website: www.hccweb.org

After one summer with Project Heritage, Janet's outlook on life changed. She completed Project Heritage's Computer-to-Career courses and secured a job with a starting salary of more than $8 an hour. Heritage Christian Center helped her with groceries, bus tokens and utility bills during the transition. One church member gave her a car, and another linked her up with quality after-school care. Janet is now working her way off welfare and has found that the church is committed to her family. Her involvement with Project Heritage has encouraged her to be all that God intended her to be.

Being a Family to the Church Member

Heritage Christian Center has a commitment to help its own church members off welfare as well. Beverly, a single mother with five children living at home, joined the church in 1994. Since she did not have her own family to help her, the church helped her with such practical needs as food and clothes for her and the children. It also met her primary need for a full-time, sustainable job by hiring her as director of the church's Graphic Arts Department. Through all these efforts, the church gave Beverly hope. Within a short amount of time, she was able to leave welfare permanently.

Heritage Christian Center continues to "stand in the gap" for Beverly. The church is supporting her in her biblical goals of being a loving mother, a responsible employee, and a Christian witness to the world. Her children attend the Christian school and the church's before-and-after-school child care program, all at a reduced rate. The men of the church have helped her with oil changes and minor car repairs through a ministry called Car Clinics. Beverly continues to be a very active member of the church which daily demonstrates the hope a church can give one of its own members.

Heritage Christian Center is committed to giving hope to all its members.

Responding to the Visitor in Need

Heritage Christian Center is committed to helping neighborhood families who come to the church for assistance. One family with four children was living in a single room in a motel when they visited the church. The father was looking for employment; the family needed food and felt hopeless. Several people in the church reached out to them with love the day they arrived. One took time to pray with the family. Another man and woman made sure their immediate needs for food and shelter were met. Through a church contact, the father obtained a job interview and was employed within a week's time. The church was interested in the long-term welfare of this family, not just in seeing them through a crisis.

With the help of the church, this family has been transformed. The father is now one of the ushers, and his wife is in the church choir. One Sunday they stood in front of the congregation and gave testimony to what God and the church had done in their lives.

Welfare Reform Round Table — from left: Arapahoe County Commissioner John Brackney, Pastor Debbie Stafford - Project Heritage, Deanna Carlson - Family Research Council and Steve Kenney - Focus on the Family.

A Blessing to the City

Heritage Christian Center and Project Heritage have built trusted relationships within their community. When many were initially opposed to having a large live-in outreach center in their city, Debbie Stafford went to various meetings to educate the community leaders about the shared goals of Project Heritage. Representatives of Heritage Christian Center and Project Heritage appeared on several local radio and television programs to educate the city about their outreach mission: to move people out of poverty with dignity, provide hope, and give families independence from government welfare.

Project Heritage now works closely with the public servants in its city. It works with the local department of social services to ensure that welfare recipients are told about its ministry and given the choice to go there for help and hope through the body of Christ. Project members have also educated their city government officials about the federal funding opportunities available to the project as a Christ-centered ministry under the Charitable Choice Provision of the welfare legislation (see the appendix). Many in the city did not know about the ministry or about some aspects of the welfare reform legislation until the church built these relationships.

In 1998, the church hosted a Welfare Reform Roundtable with community leaders and area faith-based ministries working with the poor.[60] This gathering was a way for the church to be a blessing to those on the front lines already helping the needy. Commissioner John Brackney, who is implementing welfare reform in Arapahoe County, Colorado, expressed his support of the church's work in the city:

> My county doesn't believe we have the solution to welfare reform. We are an element, but we don't believe it's our role to solve the problem, especially solve it alone. We don't have all the answers; we are devolving it right down to the churches, right down to the neighborhoods, and right back down to families and personal responsibility. We have to do it together.

Obviously you [a welfare recipient] need a job that can buy food and clothes, gas and car maintenance, and rent payments. But more than that, you need self-esteem, a sense of community, having someone care and caring for someone. No matter how well we train our government employees, they wouldn't do as good a job at that as churches do by their very design.[61]

These relationships have been pivotal in connecting welfare families with Project Heritage, and connecting Project Heritage with the poverty-fighting experts in its city.

A Congregation Transformed by God

The church found that as the poor in its community have been transformed, the church has been transformed as well. Many church members have been able to offer their professional talents and spiritual gifts in ways they have not used them before.

Julie, a single mother of three children, is a volunteer at Project Heritage. She views her volunteer work as a way to serve God, bless her church family, and be a role model to her children. She is now managing the Computer-to-Career program, helping men and women learn job skills to get off welfare. This is the first time Julie has had the opportunity to work with welfare families, and she has witnessed the transformation of many lives. She has found that though she has little experience working with those who are poor, her life-acquired skills have been a valuable resource to those she helps. She has also found that it takes a demonstrated commitment, rather than specialized skills, to build relationships with those in need.

Mary Blue, Food Services Volunteer
Heritage Christian Center

The congregation has grown as a result of the church's local missions focus. The church now knows the cultures in its own community, much as missionaries do in other countries, because the community has been drawn into its congregation. One member explained the benefits of this:

> The cultural mix is helping me to continue growing toward my goal of becoming more like Jesus. People with handicaps, various financial situations, dressed fancy or casual, all sit side by side, and are bound together with the common bond of trying to grow in our Christian walk.[62]

Becoming a community-minded church has not been easy, though. The church was predominantly a white church in the past; today, it is a multi-ethnic church with a white senior pastor. The congregation and staff of the church now reflect the ethnic diversity of the community. This transition was hard for some families, and they left the church. Yet the church was committed to trusting in God through that difficult time, and He continued to meet its needs. Today, this church bears testimonies of shattered lives rebuilt through Jesus Christ.

God's Promises

When the Israelites were called to rebuild their broken families and communities, God gave them a promise as they approached this challenge.

And if you give yourself to the hungry,

And satisfy the desire of the afflicted,

Then your light will rise in darkness,

And your gloom will become like midday.

And the Lord will continually guide you,

And satisfy your desire in scorched places,

And give strength to your bones;

And you will be like a watered garden,

And like a spring of water whose waters do not fail.

(Isaiah 58:10-11, NASB)

God has asked His church to be involved in helping the poor in all generations. His promises extend to His church today.

Chapter Six

GOD USES BROKENNESS: THE POOR WILL LEAD THE WAY

And He has said to me, "My grace is sufficient for you, for My power is perfected in weakness." Most gladly, therefore, I will rather boast about my weaknesses, so that the power of Christ may dwell in me.
2 Corinthians 12:9 (NASB)

For anyone who has the courage to enter our human sorrows deeply, there is a revelation of joy, hidden like a precious stone in the wall of a dark cave.
Henri J.M. Nouwen[63]

Becky didn't think she lacked faith in God. She had gone to church her entire life. However, at the age of 50, she was overcome with her need for "a bigger Jesus." Her husband had threatened her with divorce, and she was experiencing bouts of depression. She remembers saying to God, "My life is such a wreck. How will you ever do anything with me?"

Then Becky heard a missionary from the inner city speak at her church one Sunday. He was looking for volunteers to work with children in a housing project in her city. Becky was filled with fears at the idea. She had never been to that part of her city before, even though it was only 12 miles from her house. Yet for some reason that she couldn't understand, she felt a prompting to volunteer.

Becky has been volunteering in the inner city for 11 years now. She discipled a young woman who now leads a Bible study for children. Also, her encouragement persuaded a neighborhood ministry leader, who was on the point of giving up, to continue in the ministry. Though she had considered herself ill-equipped to help meet the needs around her, serving became a joy in that environment.

Becky found that the inner city provided the faith-stretching experiences she needed for her spiritual growth. In that atmosphere, God's attributes couldn't be hidden behind a cushion of prosperity. The Christians in the inner city were visibly needy and following God in faith. She saw miracle after miracle in the hardest circumstances: "I quickly experienced that God's love shines brightest where it is darkest. I learned to trust a bigger Jesus there." She had not experienced this radical display of God in her suburban, middle-class church.[64]

The Good Samaritan

"But a Samaritan, as he traveled, came where the man was; and when he saw him, he took pity on him. He went to him and bandaged his wounds, pouring on oil and wine. Then he put the man on his own donkey, took him to an inn and took care of him." (Luke 10:33-34)

Jesus' response to the Jewish attorney's question – "Who is my neighbor?" – displays God's truth in a perplexing way. Jesus' description of neighbor love, in fact, is quite different from what many of us imagine. Jesus could have told the attorney to love those in his neighborhood, those in his church, and those whom he knew. But His answer revealed so much more about God's love – how it is displayed and through whom it is most easily displayed.

People in Jesus' day were probably not much different from us today in that they would have expected Jesus to illustrate his story of love of neighbor with the most venerable leaders at the time – the priests and the Levites. However, that is not what happened. We recall from the story that both the priest and the Levite looked at the man on the side of the road and did nothing. It didn't matter that they should have been the ones to minister to that man – they did not.

Why did Jesus use a Samaritan, a man from the most disenfranchised group in Jewish society, to demonstrate what neighbor love looks like? The Samaritans were the least likely group to illustrate any point. They were so looked down on that the Jews would reroute their trips between Jerusalem and Jericho to avoid Samaria. The Jews believed that if a Samaritan woman entered a Jewish village, the entire village became unclean. Yet, Jesus made a Samaritan the hero of this story.

Of all the characters that Jesus introduced, the Samaritan had the shortest distance to cross to touch the injured man. He knew what it felt like to be ignored, despised, spat on, and abandoned. He certainly understood what it was like to feel utterly helpless and dependent on God's grace and mercy. He probably had seen his own people lying injured in the middle of the road before. It is clear from the story that his compassion was unfettered and immediate. His caring response was spontaneous and sprang out of his own experience.

Samaritans as God's Imagebearers

When it comes to loving our neighbor today, the story line is not much different. Christians who personally identify with the poor, the broken, the afflicted, and the displaced still best display how to love our neighbor. They can most easily show the church what neighbor love looks like.

Many Christians are used to identifying with the Good Samaritan. However, the story Jesus tells in fact elevates poor and downtrodden believers as the imagebearers of God's idea of love of neighbor. The others who love God, including the privileged Jewish attorney, are told to learn from this group. What a radical concept to think of a well-educated, socially accepted man learning from a member of a minority group, who lived in the least-esteemed neighborhood in greater Jerusalem. Yet, that is how radical neighbor love is – it empowers even the most dispossessed Christians to lead the way in loving others.

Urban and Suburban Churches

Many middle-class, suburban Christians have had a tremendous impact in ministering among the poor. Bill Millikan, a young man from the suburbs, moved to the lower east side of Manhattan, an area called "Hell's Kitchen," at age 22. He had a calling that burned within him to make a difference. Bill became the first Young Life leader in the inner city in America, ministering to countless African-American children who were in poverty. Edith, a 15-year-old with a fearless spirit, and Clark, a 17-year-old with untapped leadership skills – were two of the kids in that despairing neighborhood who were led to the Lord through Bill. Edith recalls, "I would have been dead if it wasn't for Bill. I had nothing to live for and wanted to take my life."[65]

Yet, it is not only that the inner city so desperately needs the suburban church. The suburban church also needs the Christian leaders in the poorest neighborhoods to demonstrate what love of neighbor looks like, even in the bleakest of circumstances. God's people in those circumstances carry an incredible faith and understanding of the riches of Christ Jesus. Without the inner city, the suburban church is at risk of losing its depth and perspective in outreach. Historically, a middle-class, homogeneous church outside a poor neighborhood becomes more and more separate from those living within the least-loved neighborhoods. These churches run the risk of losing perspective on what God's love fully displayed can look like. The suburban church desperately needs the poor.

Best Practices for Your Outreach Ministry

When we speak of loving our neighbors on welfare, we must recognize two very fundamental truths about this biblical concept: First, Christian outreach to the poor is most likely to be radically demonstrated by those who have been dispossessed themselves. A seminary degree or a theoretical understanding of poverty may not adequately prepare someone to pioneer the way for your church's outreach ministries to the poorest of the poor. One of the great pioneers of church-based outreach in the 20th century, John Perkins, has a third-grade education enriched by practical, time-tested experience.

Second, Christian outreach to those in need is best learned under the mentoring of the Christian leaders who have "in-the-trenches" experience with the poorest of the poor. These teachers include inner-city missionaries, minority pastors in low-income communities, and immigrant pastors in ethnic neighborhoods. There is no need for a church to reinvent the wheel in community outreach. There are many teachers who are committed to Christ in the trenches, if we would only find them. They will be able to offer "best practices" for your congregation that can touch the deepest needs.

More than 30 years ago, Edith and Clark in Hell's Kitchen both saw God give them hope and a new life in a barren neighborhood. Their personal redemptive stories have infused them with incredible vision for reaching those in the most hopeless circumstances. They, like many other Christian leaders discipled in and through poverty, continue to minister in the toughest spots across the country. Their experience, expertise, and insight have been priceless to hundreds of churches that had a God-given desire to minister to their poor neighbors but did not have this depth of perspective.[66]

A Relational Model

Transformational relationships are at the heart of the gospel. Relationships are also at the heart of ministry among the poorest of the poor. One of the ideas Edith reiterates to church leaders who join her work in Washington, D.C., is "relationships, relationships, relationships." Though this may be difficult at first, only through relationships can churches put into practice the words of 1 Corinthians 13:3: "If I give all I possess to the poor and surrender my body to the flames, but have not love, I gain nothing."

There are three groups of people with whom churches must build relationships in order to more effectively love their neighbors. Any model for ministry must be built on these types of relationships.

First, a church must build relationships with those ministers and congregations who are on the frontlines restoring the poor. Almost half of the poorest of the poor reside in major urban areas. A suburban church can begin its outreach by building a relationship with an urban ministry or church. Suburban and urban church partnerships are a vital model for churches to implement, bringing Christians together for greater impact. This model of loving requires the suburban church to humble itself and learn from those who are already at work. The suburban church has the privilege of being the supporter, refresher, helper, and equipper for the sister church and ministries laboring in the trenches.

Clark and Edith Jones, relationship builders for the kindgom, with Deanna Carlson in Washington, D.C.

More often than not, suburban and urban partnerships bring Christians of different races together. A cross-racial ministry among churches can be a radical display of love and equipping between two groups of Christians that extends beyond blessing the poor. When churches of different races come together for the benefit of a block, neighborhood, or city, they not only minister to the people served, but they also communicate a love that can come only from Christ.[67] It is a powerful example when an urban pastor from the community receives love from a suburban church and *vice versa*. This displays to the world that Christians of different races in the United States are more than equals – they are, in fact, brothers and sisters in the Lord. It is also a tremendous opportunity for a suburban church to practice the humility required for this type of partnership and for an urban church to renew its trust in the suburban church.

Second, a church must build relationships with the public servants who are already serving the poor. This starts with upholding those in your congregation who go out on the front lines daily, including those who work in the prisons, the teachers in the urban schools, social workers, city hospital workers, police officers, and even the city garbage collectors. Each of these workers is "sent out" daily to serve the needs in the community. They need the support and prayers of their churches. Additionally, they are also the primary "gatekeepers" for churches to the community in need. Remember, too, that those public servants who are not members of your church still need its prayers and support. This may include the mayor, the city planner, and the director of social services.

Third, each church, no matter its location, must continue to build intentional relationships with those who are in need. These relationships hold the promise of transforming the poor and the church. This can start with something as small as a discipleship group adopting one welfare family as a means of loving its neighbor. More often than not, poverty is synonymous with loneliness. Those most in need may not have the emotional strength to seek help from the church. The church must continue to seek them out.

Building these relationships may not be easy. To love our neighbor is a command that God intends His church to fulfill on His strength, not the church's. Otherwise, Christians would, like the world, love only our most lovable neighbors. Matthew 5:46a and 47a ask, "If you love those who love you, what reward will you get? And if you greet only your brothers, what are you doing more than others?" Loving our neighbor becomes the church's witness to the world because it is made possible through our relationship with Jesus Christ.

New Life Out of Brokenness

Welfare reform intensifies the need for churches to adopt and develop church-based ministries that will lift families out of poverty, rather than ministering to their short-term needs only. This presents a particular challenge to churches, because many of them do not have a vehicle to reach out to the needy. According to one respected ministry developer:

> The key problem I found in churches is not a lack of compassion. … Every church I worked with had the same problem. They lacked any sort of system or infrastructure. … If we can give them an infrastructure, a personnel department to link their members with children and families in the neighborhood, we can change the lives of the church members and the lives of the people who need help.[68]

These ministry vehicles are not emerging from think tanks, universities, and the political corridors of Washington, D.C. More often than not, it appears that God uses the broken to multiply the church's ministry efforts to the poor.

History is replete with stories of "least likely" individuals who have provided the vision and structures to advance church-based ministry among the needy.

> Jerry McAuley, a convicted criminal with a troubled past, started the Gospel Mission Movement at the end of the 1800s. He had never known his father, and his mother could not care for him. Consequently, his grandmother raised him. At the age of 13, he left home and chose to live with the outcasts on Water Street in the slums of the Lower East Side of New York. After a criminal conviction, he went to Sing Sing prison at the age of 19. Here, Jerry McAuley submitted his life to Jesus Christ at the age of 26. In due time, he founded the first rescue mission, Water Street Mission, in 1872 on the street where he had lived as a boy. For the next 12 years of Jerry's life, he

answered the spiritual, emotional, and physical needs of thousands of people. By 1913, more than 500 urban rescue missions were operating in the United States and Canada, using Water Street Mission as their model.[69]

In the late 1800s, Charles Crittenton, a wealthy businessman in New York City, launched the Florence Crittenton homes for unwed mothers. This ministry was born out of deep pain and brokenness. After the death of his five-year-old daughter Florence, Charles experienced a severe depression. His crisis brought him to a point of absolute surrender to Jesus Christ. Shortly after his conversion, a friend invited him to join in "rescue work" in the New York City area where the alcoholics congregated. There he met two prostitutes and promptly exhorted them to leave their lifestyles. Like some Christians today, he was taking a very individualistic "pull yourself up by your bootstraps" approach to remedying the women's situation, but he realized the hollowness of his words when he discovered that there was no place for these women to go. Using his business experience, Charles Crittenton devised a solution: He created a Christ-centered ministry to serve the need. In 1883, he launched a home for women in the neighborhood, naming it after Florence. The home was immediately overcrowded; twenty homes were opened by 1895, 45 homes were opened by 1899, and by 1933 there were 65 Florence Crittenton homes across the country.[70]

As 1 Corinthians 1:27-29 points out, God has a way of choosing "the foolish things of the world to shame the wise … the weak things of the world to shame the strong. He chose the lowly things of this world and the despised things – and the things that are not – to nullify the things that are, so that no one may boast before Him."

Where Jesus Is

Jesus is already in the inner city. Jesus is already in isolated, rural areas. There are laborers in the trenches even now ministering among the poor, praying that God would send refreshers, helpers, and equippers to increase what He is already doing. Missionary Viv Grigg states:

To find Him, we must go where He is. Did He not say, "Where I am, there shall my servant be also?" Such a search invariably leads us into the heart of poverty. For Jesus always goes to the point of deepest need. Where there is suffering, He will be there binding wounds. His compassion eternally drives Him to human need. Where there is injustice, He is there. His justice demands it. He does not dwell on the edge of the issues. He is involved, always doing battle with the fiercest of the forces of evil and powers of darkness.[71]

It is simply false to think that Jesus is not already ministering to the "deepest needs" in our low-income communities. There are dedicated, indigenous heroes giving their lives to the poor right now. Often, God raises up these individuals in response to the overwhelming injustice of their own circumstances. These individuals are used by God to ignite the hearts and minds of many to confront and remedy these and other injustices.

Consider William Seymour, an African-American pastor at the beginning of the twentieth century who enrolled in a Bible class to further his education. Due to segregation laws, he was not permitted to sit in the classroom but instead had to listen to the class outside in a hallway. In response, he started a multiracial prayer group and began to fast for days on end. During one 10-day fast, the prayer group experienced an outpouring of God's Spirit. This was the beginning of what has been recorded in the annals of history as the Azusa Street Revival of 1906. People began to flock to his neighborhood in Los Angeles to hear "Daddy Seymour" preach. One of the revival's major testimonies to the world was its display of Christian unity across racial boundaries that touched millions of believers' lives. Many in Los Angeles came to know the Lord through "Daddy Seymour."[72]

God continues to display Himself in radical ways through the afflicted in the city and in the isolated neighborhoods of America, raising up many of them to become leaders in their communities. These leaders know that "outside" churches that start their own "inner-city" projects without knowing the culture, having any urban or rural experience, or seeking the leaders' expertise will be ineffective at best and harmful at worst. The leaders have the ability to discern what help is truly needed and the tough love to provide that help. God's work in the poorest neighborhoods requires people who are humble and willing to learn, who truly desire to increase what He is already doing through these local heroes.

Joining What God Is Doing

Each church in America must decide if it is going to be a part of what God is already doing for those families most in need in our country. God is in the business of redeeming and transforming lives. His church is called to participate in this great work that brings God glory.

There are testimonies throughout the country of individuals who have been lifted out of deep poverty – spiritual, emotional, and financial – and had their entire lives radically changed by God's work displayed through His church. The stories of Viera, Maria, and Rita are not unique. Lives continue to be transformed to the greater glory of God through His church.

There are many more lives that still need the "good news" of God's grace and the love of God's people. We understand that welfare families, in particular, need what the church alone can provide in these critical days. Due to numerous factors, including the effects of the welfare state, current-day welfare reform, the growth of materialism, and suburbaniza-

A meeting of esteemed urban ministry leaders in Detroit (that FRC was invited to join), including Jerald January (far left), pioneer of Compassion International's USA program.

tion within the church, many of the "hidden poor" in our communities continue in their isolation. Many continue to suffer without hope for a better tomorrow.

God wants to use you and your church to love and restore your neighbors, no matter where you are situated. You may be like Becky, a suburbanite living outside a low-income neighborhood. In Becky's church, the welfare mother is not likely to be sitting in the next pew. Or you may be like the Good Samaritan, living inside a community that desperately needs help and hope. It isn't hard to imagine the Good Samaritan living in inner-city Washington, D.C., or Chicago. It would be impossible not to know someone on welfare in congregations there.

God continues to look for yielded people from all walks of life to accomplish His purposes. He doesn't need Ph.D.s, MSWs, and M.Div.s in urban ministry to reach the poor. Rather, God needs individuals who have experienced brokenness before Him and restoration through Him, and who are now yielded to Him. These are the people God pours out to restore our broken communities and our broken families.

Ironically, it is our inadequacies that qualify us to help restore our neighbors. Ministry to the poor starts with knowing what we don't have outside of God. We then become vessels to be used for God's purposes. We find our own brokenness visibly displayed through those who are in need, and they serve as constant reminders of our own state of dependence before God. We, like Becky, can see God working through our weaknesses to meet deep, deep needs.

God has a plan for His church that is bigger than any of us can imagine. Whoever we are and wherever we live, God wants to use us and our churches to reach "the hidden poor" in our communities. He knows where He wants us, and He will direct our steps. He will not waste one yielded heart, one yielded church through which to display His glory.

Are we now going to be a part of what God has already begun with welfare families in America?

Thy lovingkindness, O LORD, extends to the heavens,
Thy faithfulness reaches to the skies.

How precious is Thy lovingkindness, O God!

And the children of men take refuge
in the shadow of Thy wings.

They drink their fill in the abundance
of Thy house;

And Thou dost give them to drink
of the river of Thy delights.

For with Thee

is the fountain of life;

In Thy light we see light. Psalm 36:5-9 (NAS)

Photos taken by Dan Kim, a volunteer with Little Lights Urban Ministries in Washington, D.C. Used by permission.

Part 2

LOVING MY NEIGHBOR

The following pages will introduce you to ways that you can increase your church's out-reach to your neighbors on welfare. As you prayerfully seek God's calling for your church, you will see that you are not alone. There are many individuals and ministries who can help you join what God is already doing for your neighbors in need.

"A man was going down from Jerusalem to Jericho, when he fell into the hands of robbers. They stripped him of his clothes, beat him and went away, leaving him half dead. A priest happened to be going down the same road, and when he saw the man, he passed by on the other side. So too, a Levite, when he came to the place and saw him, passed by on the other side. But a Samaritan, as he traveled, came where the man was; and when he saw him he took pity on him. He went to him pouring on oil and wine. Then he put the man on his own donkey, took him to an inn and took care of him. The next day he took out two silver coins and gave them to the innkeeper. 'Look after him,' he said, 'and when I return, I will reimburse you for any extra expense you may have.'" (Luke 10:30-35)

Chapter Seven

SIXTY-SIX WAYS TO LOVE YOUR NEIGHBOR OFF WELFARE

L isted below are a number of ways your church can love a family off welfare into full-time employment. Once you prayerfully decide what you can do, call your county department of social services and tell the director of your church's intent. There are a number of Christ-centered ministries that can also help your church begin mentoring a welfare family or start an employment ministry to move welfare recipients successfully into jobs (see Chapter 8). Every church can start a ministry or offer supports that address one or more of the four key needs of welfare families — mentoring, employment, transportation and child care.

All of these ideas assume that you are in a reciprocal relationship with a family moving off welfare. You can expect everyone involved to be changed by this relationship.

If your church is not located near the people you are trying to serve, we suggest that you partner with a church or ministry in their neighborhood.

MENTORING

1 *Love a welfare family.* Build a relationship between their family and yours. Show them how valuable they are by investing in their lives.

2 *Adopt a welfare family.* See Chapter 8 for a list of Christ-centered ministries that can help your church establish a mentoring ministry for families.

3 *Provide a "Mom's Day Off" for a former welfare mother in transition.* Ask people in your church to assist with watching her kids, doing the dishes, cleaning her home, and doing laundry.

4 *Celebrate milestones with a welfare family.* Throw a party when a newly employed welfare mom or dad receives the first paycheck.

5 *Invite a welfare family to join in your church's activities.* Invite them to your neighborhood Bible study. Ask them to join your prayer chain. Personally invite them to your church social events, and make sure these events are affordable for everyone.

6 *Mentor a welfare mom or dad* in punctuality, time management, problem solving, conflict management, responsibility, and job retention.[73]

7 *Invite a welfare mom to share her testimony during a Sunday morning service.* Help her write out her testimony about how God has been faithful to her. Encourage her to tell her story to many others.

8 *Invite a welfare mom or dad who is a member of your church to serve.* Ask him or her to do something that requires little time but would build self-esteem (e.g., joining the choir, being an usher, being a greeter).

9 *Provide support groups and individual counseling at your church for welfare families* dealing with issues such as parenting, anger, harmful relationships, domestic violence, stress, and marital problems.[74]

10 *Offer a class at your church on budgeting.*[75] Then teach a welfare mom or dad how to go grocery shopping on a budget.

11 *Teach a welfare mom or dad how to balance a checkbook.* Then go to the bank with him or her to open up a checking account.

12 *Provide a practical health and nutrition class at your church.* Talk about how to prepare nutritious and low-cost meals.

13 *Call a newly employed welfare mom or dad a couple of times a week to see how he or she is doing.* If needed, give him or her a wake-up call in the morning for work.

EMPLOYMENT

14 *Take a welfare mom or dad to a few low-cost clothing stores.* Help him or her pick out an interview outfit that is within his or her budget. Provide the shoes, nylons, or accessories that he or she may not be able to afford. Teach a free "Dress for Success" and etiquette seminar through your church.

15 *Tell a welfare family about job openings.* Encourage your friends to do the same.

16   *Assist a welfare mom or dad with writing a résumé.* Set up a typewriter or computer at your church for résumé writing.

17   *Teach a welfare mom or dad job search skills* such as utilizing newspapers, employment agencies, and personal networks (such as your church) to obtain employment.

18   *Hold a job fair at your church for welfare moms and dads.* Invite employment agencies and area businesses to host tables. Establish a resource network for current job listings in your community.[76]

19   *Ask your pastor to be a personal reference for employment for a welfare mom or dad your church knows.* Offer a letter of reference to a welfare family you know quite well.[77]

20   *Be an interview coach for a welfare mom or dad.* Set up a mock interviewing studio with a video camera for interviewing practice.

21   *Teach a welfare mom or dad how to fill out a job application.* Assist him or her to gather items that may be needed (i.e., birth certificate, ID card, and social security card).[78]

22   *Teach a welfare mom or dad job follow-up skills,* including sending a thank-you letter after an interview.

23   *Invite a transitioning welfare mom or dad to "shadow" you at work.*[79]

24   *Provide a no-interest loan, expertise, and support for a transitioning welfare recipient who has the skills to start his or her own business.*[80]

25   *Assist a newly employed welfare recipient with his or her tax return.* Set up a tax clinic at your church for church volunteers to teach former welfare families how to fill out their returns. Make sure they claim the earned income credit.[81]

26   *Identify potential employers for hard-to-employ welfare recipients* (former prisoners, handicapped, recovering addicts, etc.).

27   *Drive a transitioning welfare mom or dad to a job interview.* Talk about how it went in the car on the way home.

28   *Offer an individual or group Bible study* on self-esteem to transitioning welfare moms and dads.

29   *Ask professionals in the church to teach vocational skills classes.*[82]

30 *Offer a computer literacy course at your church.*

31 *Tutor a welfare mom or dad in additional English, writing or math skills.*

32 *Offer a literacy program at your church.*[83]

33 *Hire a welfare recipient to work at your church or workplace.*[84]

34 *Be a job cheerleader for the newly employed,* especially when they are discouraged or facing challenges with their employers.

CHILD CARE

35 *Assist welfare moms and dads in finding appropriate day-care for their children.* Inform them of their right to choose a religious day care provider through a voucher program.

36 *If your church provides child care, encourage it to accept government vouchers to make your center accessible to welfare families.*[85]

37 *Provide start-up kits for welfare recipients starting home-based day-care centers.*[86]

38 *Set up non-traditional child care for newly employed welfare moms and dads.*[87] Short-term child care is needed for job interviews, training, etc.; after-hours child care for parents who work non-traditional hours; and special care for children with minor illnesses.[88] Infant care can also be difficult to locate.

39 *Be an emergency babysitter for a newly employed* welfare mom or dad.

40 *Provide child care for welfare families as they move into or out of homes or apartments.*

41 *Provide free child care for participants in mentoring programs, support groups, employment ministries, etc.,* taking place at your church.

TRANSPORTATION

42 *Set up an alternative transportation system to get city residents out to the suburbs for jobs.* Be creative.[89]

43 *Purchase and give out bus tokens for transportation to job interviews.*[90]

44 *Establish a car clinic* where low-income families can bring their cars for repair.[91]

45   *Ask your church members to give their old cars to families in the church who need transportation.* Ask volunteer mechanics in the church to perform needed repairs to the cars.[92]

46   *Ask used car dealers to donate cars to newly employed welfare recipients in your church.* Encourage the new owner of the car, once on his or her feet, to give it to another transitioning welfare recipient.[93]

47   *Start a bus, vanpool (using the church bus or van), or carpool* to take welfare moms and dads to work.[94]

48   *Give a welfare mom or dad rides to and from work and church.*[95]

49   *Help a welfare mom or dad obtain a driver's license.* Provide driver's training classes.

50   *Subsidize the first year of car insurance* for a welfare family.

51   *Contract with a local bus service to take transitioning welfare moms and dads to and from their jobs.* Make this a ministry of your church.[96]

ADDITIONAL WAYS TO HELP

52   *Provide voice mail and post office boxes through your church* for transitioning welfare recipients who do not have street addresses and/or phones.[97]

53   *Start a clearinghouse ministry* to match church volunteers with the needs in the community (see Chapter 8 for two examples of clearinghouse ministries).

54   *Develop a referral directory of church-based and parachurch ministries in your community that work with the poor.* Give this to your county department of social services.[98]

55   *Open a crisis intervention line for welfare moms and dads in your area to call if they have crises that might interfere with getting to work or keeping jobs.*[99]

56   *Ask your church to host a Christian 12-step program for drug- or alcohol-addicted welfare recipients.*[100]

57   *Develop a church hospitality network* to house families one week at a time.[101]

58   *Identify landlords in the congregation who might be willing to provide low-cost housing* with supplemental assistance from the church or members of the congregation.

59　*Consider purchasing an apartment and/or house to provide low-cost housing for needy families in the community.* Strict requirements for life-skill improvements and job training could be required in order to live in the apartments.[102]

60　*Develop "moving teams" to assist welfare families without support systems when they need to move.*

61　*Develop a furniture bank* to provide household furniture for welfare families.

62　*Develop "handy man" teams to provide minor home repairs for welfare families.*

63　*Develop "cleaning teams" to assist welfare families as they move into or out of homes or apartments.*

64　*Provide a rental deposit and first month's rent for families moving towards independence.* Perhaps a home-missions team could establish a certain number of families per month or year that it is willing to sponsor. Screening and a motivation for life change could be part of the decision-making process to qualify.[103]

65　*Provide meals for welfare families during moving or other transition times.*

66　*Teach a welfare family how to qualify for a first-time home loan.*

Chapter Eight

CHRIST-CENTERED WELFARE-TO-WORK MINISTRIES

The following organizations provide face-to-face assistance to welfare recipients through Christ-centered parachurch ministries. Each has a reputation as a biblically based ministry rooted in love for the poor. Each has taken an innovative approach to helping welfare families move into jobs quickly or to equipping churches to reach out to their neighbors on welfare. Each has experienced some measure of success in helping the poor in its neighborhood.

These ministries are listed here as teaching examples for churches across the country. All are happy to assist any church in setting up similar programs. Of course, we encourage churches to first support existing ministries and neighborhood leaders before starting their own ministries. Starting one's own ministry is necessary when nothing else is available.

The ministries here are divided into three categories: mentoring, employment and clearinghouse. All three types form a necessary foundation in every county or region in America for advancing church-based ministry among the poor.

MENTORING

Mentoring ministries — This type of ministry helps an individual or a team from a church to "adopt" a welfare family. A mentoring ministry allows a welfare family to build needed friendships and networks that are crucial to finding and retaining jobs. The adoptee is referred by social services on a voluntary basis, and the people who adopt are church volunteers committed to building relationships with welfare families. In fact, mentoring ministries are based on building long-term relationships.

CHRISTIAN WOMEN'S JOB CORPS

A ministry of Woman's Missionary Union
Trudy Johnson, National Director
P.O. Box 83001
Birmingham, AL 35283-0010
Phone: (800) 968-7301
Fax: (205) 995-4846
E-mail: cwjc@wmu.org
Website: www.wmu.com

Founded March 1, 1997, Christian Women's Job Corps is a ministry of the Woman's Missionary Union of the Southern Baptist Convention, the largest Protestant women's organization in the world. The purpose of the Christian Women's Job Corps is to provide a Christian context in which women in need are equipped for life and employment, and a missions context in which women help women. Women who sign up for the program enroll in CWJC classes, generally for 10 weeks, and are matched with mentors. Most are employed but need support to maintain their jobs. CWJC began as a response to WMU staff members coming face to face with the poor in the Appalachian region of Kentucky in 1993.

Two volunteers experience a closer relationship with Christ through their work with Christian Women's Job Corps.

Each CWJC site is independently run and customized to the needs in the community. All CWJC sites utilize the following key elements: a mentor for every client, Bible study, a covenant between clients and mentors, networking, needs assessments of communities and clients, state or local advisory councils, certification training through the CWJC national certification program, and evaluation. Most women in need are referred by county social services and housing services. All churches, not just Southern Baptist churches, are asked to mentor women through the CWJC sites in their communities. Each site leader must take CWJC National Certification Training (16 hours) which includes courses on understanding poverty, welfare reform, recruiting volunteers, resource development, legal issues, grant writing, and evaluation. Ongoing training and a training video will be offered nationally and regionally through Woman's Missionary Union.

As of January 1999, there were 50 operational sites for CWJC, located in Washington, D.C.; Virginia; Illinois; Georgia; Tennessee; South Carolina; Alabama; Mississippi; New Mexico; North Dakota; and California. More than 1,000 women have been helped nationally, with more than 25 returning to the program as mentors. WMU pilot projects were conducted from January 1996 through March 1, 1997, in York, South Carolina; San Antonio, Texas; Chicago, Illinois; Bismarck, North Dakota; and Washington, D.C. In 1998, 350 new site coordinators were trained in the second National Certification Training. The Department of Social Services for Madison County, Alabama, has declared CWJC its faith-based welfare-to-work initiative. In May 1997, CWJC was recognized by the White House as a viable program for assisting women in the transition from welfare to work.

Christian Women's Job Corps will send any interested church a video and introductory packet on its ministry.

FAITH AND FAMILIES: THE GOVERNOR'S WELFARE AGENDA

Reverend Ronald Moore, Director
5201 Cedar Park, Suite K
Jackson, MS 39206
Phone: (601) 957-5125
Fax: (601) 957-9934
E-mail: ronnierkm@aol.com

Initiated in 1994 by then-Governor Kirk Fordice, Faith and Families is a voluntary partnership among the Mississippi Department of Human Services and local churches and synagogues to help welfare recipients become self-sufficient. It was the first state effort in the country to match transitioning welfare families with churches for additional support. It seeks to facilitate the faith community's commitment to the spiritual and physical well-being of the poor and to foster the one-on-one relationships that welfare families need and government cannot provide.

Faith and Families serves as a bridge organization between the Department of Human Services (DHS) and participating churches. DHS notifies all TANF recipients of their option to be paired with a church for additional, voluntary support. Churches that express interest in adopting welfare families are given blind profiles of one welfare family per church. Once a church commits to helping a particular family, Faith and Families facilitates the arrangement among the welfare family, the church, and DHS. An adopting church will help the family determine what it needs and plan a course of action. The church then chooses its own team and strategy to work with its family. Faith and Families provides ongoing support to churches through four field coordinators who contact the participating churches monthly and the welfare families biweekly. Each adopting church is asked to commit a minimum of six months to a welfare family.

> "Stronger Hope Baptist Church, a congregation of 300 moderate-income African-American families, has helped 19 welfare recipients find jobs and a new way of life through Faith and Families."
>
> Amy Sherman, "Little Miracles: How Churches Are Responding to Welfare Reform," *The American Enterprise*, Jan/Feb. 1998, p. 68.

Since Faith and Families' first pilot project in 1995, more than 800 churches in Mississippi have adopted welfare families. Over 400 of the adopted welfare families are now self-sufficient. The Department of Human Services has referred more than 1,100 volunteering welfare families to Faith and Families. Faith and Families has been replicated in Indiana, Texas, Louisiana and Tennessee. Efforts are in development in Georgia and Arkansas. Faith and Families will send an introductory packet and a 50-minute church training video to anyone interested in replicating their program. They are happy to share their experience with callers as well.

GOOD SAMARITAN MINISTRIES

Janet DeYoung, Executive Director
513 E. 8th Street, Suite 25
Holland, MI 49423
Phone: (616) 392-7159
Fax: (616) 392-5889
E-mail: jdeyoung@macatawa.org
Website: www.mibusiness.com/gsm

Good Samaritan Ministries is a private, nonprofit human service ministry with a mission to equip local churches to meet community needs. Good Samaritan Ministries is known nationally for its expertise in building intermediary structures and supports between the Christian community and the social services community. GSM has been partnering with local churches in the Holland/Zeeland area since 1969 and has established a solid working relationship with local churches and private agencies, as well as with the Ottawa County Family Independence Agency (formerly the Department of Social Services).

GSM's church-based mentoring curriculum is called "Building Transformational Relationships with Low-Income Families." It includes such topics as budgeting, goal-setting, self-esteem, and managing day-to-day problems. GSM's professional staff trains small teams from local churches who agree to mentor welfare families or low-income families for six months to one year. Each church mentor receives four hours of initial orientation and training; additional training is provided as needed. GSM supplies a professionally trained case manager to provide ongoing support to the church team.

> "[Governor John] Engler attributed much of the county's unprecedented success to the faith community."
>
> Jon Jeter, "Michigan County Finds Jobs for All Welfare Recipients," *The Washington Post,* September 16, 1997, p. A5.

Since 1996, Good Samaritan Ministries has contracted with Michigan's Welfare Reform Initiative, Project Zero, to provide ongoing support to welfare recipients after they are placed in jobs. Since mid-1996, the Ottawa County Family Independence Agency has referred over 200 welfare recipients to Good Samaritan Ministries (and three partner Love INC organizations) for linkage with ministry teams from local churches. In 1997, approximately 70 churches helped 80 families meet state welfare-to-work guidelines in just over a year through GSM's partnership with Project Zero. Through these combined efforts, Ottawa County, Michigan, became the first locality in the nation to move every able-bodied welfare recipient into a job.

Note: The former executive director of Good Samaritan Ministries, Bill Raymond, established FaithWorks Consulting Services in June 1998. FaithWorks assists churches, community organizations, and governments to establish intermediary structures and supports to sustain church-based mentoring ministries within social service delivery systems. Please call Good Samaritan Ministries for contact information for FaithWorks.

A Commited Church Makes National Headlines

"Twenty-seven and the single mother of five young children, [Gloria] Garcia was homeless and jobless when her caseworker asked her ... if she would like to be coupled with mentors from one of the area churches. She agreed, and parishioners at Hardewyk Christian Reformed Church took up Garcia's cause. Hampered by day care problems, Garcia lost her job after failing to show up for work several times. But Ginny Weerstra, a parishioner at Hardewyk, put in a call to the temporary employment service where Garcia had worked and asked them to give her a second chance. 'I just told her that Gloria had people behind her now when she runs into trouble.' ... The employer agreed. ... One parishioner, an auto mechanic, accompanied Garcia when she went car shopping, the first time in her life when she had done so. ... Weerstra helped Garcia find an affordable home. Other parishioners babysit her kids if she needs a breather and have helped her make a budget. ... Garcia ... said that merely knowing someone else cares has made all the difference in her chaotic world. 'It just seems like whenever I've had a problem they're there for me,' Garcia said."

Jon Jeter, "A Homespun Safety Net: Michigan Community Finds Jobs for All on Welfare," *The Washington Post*, October 8, 1997, p. A1.

LOVE INC (IN THE NAME OF CHRIST) - RELATIONAL MINISTRIES

(In partnership with World Vision USA)
Pattie Juarez, Love INC Coordinator
P.O. Box 9716, Mail Stop 312
Federal Way, WA 98063-9716
Phone: (800) 777-5277
Fax: (253) 815-3341
E-mail: pjuarez@wvus.org
Website: www.worldvision.org/worldvision/wvususfo.nsf/stable/usfo

In 1998, Love INC (see "Clearinghouse Ministries," p. 91) added a program called Relational Ministries to its efforts. Relational Ministries is a program for local churches to minister to welfare families through relationships. It was developed so that local churches would have a system in place to address the long-term needs of the welfare families that are referred to them through Love INC. It is based on an original, detailed mentoring curriculum designed for Love INC affiliates and local churches. The mentoring program addresses the following areas: intake forms (assessment, agreement and confidentiality) for the Love INC clearinghouse, budget counseling, Bible study, financial freedom training for children, and managing a bank account. Relational Ministries is based on a 6- to 10-person team from a church adopting a welfare family and establishing a contract to help them reach their shared goals.

Love INC is training the Love INC program directors through both the national World Vision Conference (Spring) and regional training on Relational Ministries. The Love INC program directors will lead 6- to 12-week training programs for local church leaders to start Relational Ministries in their churches. While this is new, it looks promising. Love INC headquarters in Federal Way, Washington, can direct your church to a Love INC program director who can conduct Relational Ministries training for your church.

Christ-centered mentoring relationships promise to transform both the giver and the receiver.

MOPS INTERNATIONAL (MOTHERS OF PRESCHOOLERS)

P.O. Box 102200
Denver, CO 80250-2200
Phone: (888) 910-MOPS
Fax: (303) 733-5770
E-mail: info@MOPS.org
Website: www.mops.org

MOPS International, Inc., was formed in 1973 to assist churches in providing Christ-centered ministry to mothers of preschoolers. The MOPS groups are ministries of each local church supported by MOPS International. MOPS groups are led by the mothers themselves, with the help of a MOPS Mentor, an older woman. MOPS groups focus on instruction related to the unique needs of womanhood, motherhood, and family relationships, based on biblical principles. Each MOPS group must obtain a charter through MOPS International, Inc. Substantive resource materials and training opportunities are available for charter members.

Urban MOPS

Urban MOPS was developed in 1993 by Shelly Travis at Jubilee Church in Denver.

Urban MOPS provides weekly meetings where mothers can participate in a time of teaching and discussion, a creative activity, or life-skill training. Life-skill training can include personal development, budgeting, nutrition, and workplace issues. Urban MOPS is designed to minister to urban welfare mothers transitioning into full-time employment.

> "MOPS should be a revolving door that invites women into a safe and encouraging place where restoration can begin, and then sends them out again to care for themselves and their children."
>
> Shelly Travis, MOPS brochure

Suburban MOPS groups are encouraged to partner with inner-city groups to assist with practical needs, such as child care, and to build relationships between women. As of early 1999, there are 11 Urban MOPS groups in six states. Charter members receive Urban MOPS Manuals.

NEW FOCUS

Jenny Forner, Executive Director
6837 Lake Michigan Drive
P.O. Box 351
Allendale, MI 49401
Phone: (616) 895-5356
Fax: (616) 895-5355
E-mail: jenny@newfocus.org
Website: www.newfocus.org

New Focus's mission statement reads: "You Can Make a Change in Someone's Welfare." New Focus, founded in 1994 by Jenny Forner, is a church-based relational system that allows churches to utilize "knock on the door" requests to move the poor to financial independence and spiritual growth through long-term relationships. The New Focus relational system consists of developmental steps that the church provides for those who voluntarily enroll. All those who "knock on the door" of the church asking for money are invited to attend an introduction on New Focus to determine whether they want to enroll. Each person who enrolls is matched with a small group from the church that develops a long-term plan to help the participant leave welfare. The plan includes enrollment in a 12-week financial freedom class, followed by participation in a Compassion Circle. The Compassion Circle provides ongoing friendship and support for the individual as he or she takes steps towards financial independence.

New Focus provides three-day training sessions for individual congregations interested in using the New Focus system in their benevolence ministries. This training covers poverty sensitivity, volunteer management, how to motivate others, how to teach money management, how to develop "compassion circles," how to fund the ministry, how to work with other churches, and how to accurately assess an individual's needs. New Focus has trained 37 churches, belonging to 17 denominations, in 13 states. Some of their successes to date include a church in Minnesota that has helped 52 people from 19 families with 13,800 hours of volunteer time, and a church in Grand Rapids, Michigan, that has served 80 families with 150 volunteers.

> "In three months we have enrolled six families in NEW FOCUS. We have seen not only these families receive much-needed help and support, but also 100 members of our congregation became actively involved in the lives of these families some way. It has permitted us to put names and faces on what in the past has simply been called benevolence and outreach. NEW FOCUS has helped open our eyes to specific needs in our community and encouraged us to jump in and get our hands dirty in ministry."
>
> Herb and Marla Van Iddekinge, New Focus coordinators at Faith Christian Reformed Church in Holland, Michigan. From the New Focus brochure.

ONE CHURCH ONE FAMILY

Bonita Williams, Executive Director
One Church One Family Foundation
Community Services Building
100 W. 10th Street, Suite 106
Wilmington, DE 19801
Phone: (302) 777-7270
Fax: (302) 777-7276
E-mail: ocof@dca.net

One Church One Family was founded in July 1997 as a direct response to the 1996 welfare reform law. OCOF believes that welfare reform places a special responsibility on churches to minister to welfare families in transition. Its mission is to encourage every church in Delaware to adopt a family in need and assist that family to become self-sufficient through mentoring and Christian discipleship. The Foundation matches volunteering welfare families with willing congregations, who are asked to commit to adopting families for a minimum of six months. OCOF provides four-hour training sessions for church volunteers and participant families at area churches. The Delaware Department of Health and Social Services includes the One Church One Family programs on its referral list for welfare families.

As of early 1999, 70 families had enrolled in OCOF, and 57 Delaware churches are participating. OCOF can assist churches across the state by explaining their model and sending them an introductory packet on mentoring.

"In Dover, Grace Presbyterian Church and Calvary Baptist Church are jointly mentoring their second family in six months since they connected with the One Church One Family project.

"The two churches are held up as an example of what churches can do together. Grace Church, with 700 active, mostly white members, is part of the religiously conservative Presbyterian Church of America. Calvary, a large African-American independent congregation in Dover, is headed by a registered Democrat. Their pastors have a 20-year difference in ages, but they share the same attitude about the duty of churches in the new welfare-to-work age. ...

"For smaller congregations such as Powerhouse Church of God in Christ in Clayton, it comes down to the kind of one-on-one counseling that the Rev. Dwayne Bull found himself doing for a homeless, unmarried couple who arrived by bus in Delaware from New Jersey last summer with 14 children.

"Bull's congregation gave the clan food, clothes, and money. They arranged car pools to get the adults to work and the entire family to church on Sunday.

"The father in the large family from New Jersey now has been working at the same job for four months, a church member gave him a 1980 Cadillac and Bull taught him how to set up a bank account.

"But the tiny Pentecostal church has its financial limits. So the 2,000-member Calvary Assembly of God Church ... has members standing by to build bunk beds."

Rhonda R. Graham, "Churches Rise to New Challenges," *The (Wilmington, Del.) News Journal,* Tuesday, April 21, 1998, pp. D1-D2

PUTTING FAMILIES FIRST FOUNDATION

Lisa VanRiper, Executive Director
Whitney Yarborough, Deputy Director
North Greenville College
P.O. Box 9022
Greenville, SC 29604-9022
Phone: (864) 2-FAMILY (message center) or (864) 977-2001
Website: www.worthwhile.com/familiesfirst

Putting Families First Foundation's mission is to encourage every church, synagogue, civic club, and organization in South Carolina to adopt a welfare family and help that family make the transition to independence. In May 1996, then-Governor and Mrs. David Beasley authorized the use of the governor's private inaugural funds to start a statewide foundation that would collaborate with the department of social services, faith-based organizations, community agencies, and businesses. The Foundation's ultimate goal is to support welfare reform by helping welfare recipients secure jobs; take responsibility for the lives of their family members; and, within two years, leave the welfare rolls.

The Foundation is asking churches to become involved specifically by building long-term relationships that fulfill the spiritual, emotional and material needs of families in poverty. Churches form "partnering teams" to mentor welfare families for 12 months. Each team includes a group coordinator, a family mentor, a financial planner, and a special events coordinator who plans a special occasion at least once a month for every family. The Foundation works as closely with a church as the church's needs dictate. It sends a representative to form the partnering team, assess the strengths of the church, and connect the church with a welfare family that matches the church's strengths. Foundation staffers will call the church bimonthly for progress reports and are available daily to answer questions.

As of December 1998, the Foundation has been instrumental in the adoption of 250 families on welfare in South Carolina. Two hundred eighty-one churches and civic groups have entered the partnering process with the Foundation. Additionally, the Foundation has formed statewide partnerships with five major denominations. Staffers have presented their vision to more than 700 groups in South Carolina. The Putting Families First program model has been replicated conceptually in Missouri (Putting Families First/J.C. Can), Florida (Community Hands) and Washington state. The Foundation invites states, counties, denominations, and churches to visit in order to learn their strategies and replicate them. Its consulting team is available to travel to other states to help them kick off their efforts.

A Success Story of Putting Families First

There are many success stories among the adopted families. In one success story, a Sunday School class in Florence, SC adopted a single mother and her four children. Class members helped the mother secure a full-time job at a local hospital, but she had no way to get to work. So, class members took turns carpooling her to her job, which began at 6:45 each morning.

When a sales manager at a local car dealership heard of the mother's efforts to become self-sufficient, he donated a 1989 Chevrolet Corsica to her family. Thus, the mother was able to sustain her employment.

STEP (STRATEGIES TO ELEVATE PEOPLE)

Marcie Nobles, Executive Director
436 Calhoun Street
Richmond, VA 23220
Phone: (804) 648-7552
Fax: (804) 648-5730
E-mail: steprichmond@mindspring.com
Website: www.wepc.org (site of West End Presbyterian Church; see "missions/STEP")

STEP Richmond began at a Christian conference organized by Harv Oostdyk (see poem, p. 136,137), where members of two suburban churches and an urban church felt God lay a burden on their hearts during a session at which E.V. Hill was speaking. STEP started in 1983 with six suburban churches focusing their resources on Richmond's public housing project, Gilpin Court. At the time, Gilpin Court was characterized by large-scale drug use, a very high homicide rate, generational welfare dependency, fatherlessness, and very low educational attainment.

STEP could be called a nonprofit that facilitates partnership between suburban and urban neighborhoods for the transformation of all involved. Its ministry among Gilpin Court families is based on four objectives: 1) supporting the urban church, 2) supporting institutions already serving the city, 3) directly ministering to individuals in need, and 4) designing plans to meet unmet institutional and personal needs.

STEP continues to modify its strategies to meet the changing needs of Gilpin Court families. In 1992, STEP started the "I Am Academy" to provide vocational training for parents leaving welfare to go to work, and "Family Share Teams," Christian small groups to mentor and encourage students. In 1997, due to changes in Virginia welfare policy, STEP replaced the "I Am Academy" with the Jobs Partnership curriculum from Raleigh (see "Employment Ministries," p. 86) to move parents into jobs more quickly. The "Family Share Teams" have developed into one-to-one mentoring, which continues to provide ongoing relational support to Gilpin Court families moving from welfare to work.

STEP today is a partnership of more than 30 suburban and urban churches actively involved in the lives of families in Gilpin Court. Since 1997, 92 percent of the families who have completed its Jobs Partnership program have found jobs. The graduates continue to be a part of the STEP urban-suburban church family. Over half the Gilpin Court tenant council now is made up of Jobs Partnership graduates.

STEP's neighborhood-based strategies have been incorporated into various models across the country, including Richmond's GREAT (Greater Employment Assistance Training Program) welfare-to-work mentoring initiative. Members are available to speak at conferences on successful urban/suburban church partnerships and mentoring. They are always happy to talk with interested churches about their model and how they adjust to meet the needs of Gilpin Court families.

Dr. Amy Sherman, expert on church-based mentoring, notes that successful church mentoring programs for welfare recipients share the following characteristics:

1) They employ a team approach, rather than [relying solely on] one-to-one mentoring. This reduces the chances of volunteer burnout, enlarges program participants' network of contacts, and allows volunteers to find their particular niche in the ministry.

2) They have clearly defined expectations for both the church members and the welfare recipients.

3) They are marked by regular, face-to-face, structured contact between the volunteers and the participants. They do not rely on spontaneous interaction.

4) They demand individual responsibility.[104]

EMPLOYMENT MINISTRY

Employment ministries — In the truest sense "welfare-to-work," these ministries include job placement, readiness, and training programs that integrate a Christ-centered worldview. All are led by Christian leaders from various walks of life and employ both volunteers and professional staff to execute their missions. The chief aim of employment ministries is to move welfare recipients into jobs in which they will be successful. These ministries rely on financial and volunteer support from churches. They may rely also on mentoring ministries for ongoing support for their participants who have begun jobs.

A Crisis Pregnancy Center Starts a Job Training Program

"In 1991 I was having a discussion with one of my pregnancy counselors, Bob Blakeslee, who was a retired IBM executive. Bob had been counseling for a year and we were lamenting how we were often seeing the same women coming for pregnancy tests and yet their lives were still in disarray. Bob said if we ever decided we wanted to offer these women a chance at learning a skill so they could gain some financial independence, he would be willing to teach computer skills.

"Like most pregnancy centers, we didn't have extra funds to begin a program like that. The idea remained just that, an idea, until we heard about a local radio station which offered community service grants to nonprofit agencies. I called the station, pitched the idea, they loved it and funded it!"

Gail Tierney, executive director of Rockville Pregnancy Center, remembers the beginning of Computer Moms.

Bob Blakeslee, founder of Computer Moms, and
Darlene, a Computer Moms graduate

COMPUTER MOMS

Gail Tierney, Executive Director
Rockville Pregnancy Center
12022 Parklawn Drive
Rockville, MD 20852
Phone: (301) 770-4444
Fax: (301) 770-0538

Started in 1991 by a crisis pregnancy center director and a businessman, Computer Moms is a computer skills training program for pregnant women and mothers of young children who demonstrate financial need. The program, sponsored by the Rockville Pregnancy Center (RPC), has become a model for crisis pregnancy centers across the country. It was developed to provide a means for mothers and their children to step out of the cycle of poverty.

Computer Moms focuses on job readiness and job training by teaching mothers basic computer skills. Enrollees can be married or single, and they must be motivated to seek employment upon graduation from the Computer Moms Program. Students learn basic keyboarding skills and receive instruction in Microsoft Word and Excel. Computer Moms relies on church volunteers to teach individualized computer classes. Workshops are also taught twice monthly by experts in the community on topics such as job applications, interviews, employment opportunities, proper workplace attitude and behavior, résumé preparation, makeup and clothing tips, and basic grammar. Once the women graduate, they may shop in the "Dress for Success" corner, to which women in the community have donated career clothing and accessories. Graduates also receive certificates of completion from Computer Moms.

As of early 1999, Computer Moms had trained 68 women, over 80 percent of whom were working in jobs related to the Computer Moms training. This was done with only four computers and seven teachers training eight students per day. In 1993, the program was named a "Point of Light" by former President Bush. In 1998, the program was presented as a national model at Focus on the Family's national conference for pregnancy centers. The Rockville Pregnancy Center has a manual for replication of its program called *Computer Moms: A How-To Manual for Pregnancy Centers*.

Ed Anderson, Computer Moms teacher, and Christy, graduate

NATIONAL JOBS PARTNERSHIP

Skip Long, Executive Director
4208 Six Forks Road, Building II, Suite 320
Raleigh, NC 27609
Phone: (919) 571-8614
Fax: (919) 786-4912
E-mail: tjp@ccmangum.com
Websites: www.ccmangum.com/tjp/ or
www.jobspartnership.org/[105]

Jobs Partnership was formed in 1996 out of the friendship between Chris Mangum, CEO of a Raleigh-based construction firm, and Donald McCoy, pastor of a small, mostly African-American church. Mangum contracted to pave the church parking lot and consequently formed a fast friendship with the pastor. Out of this relationship, the idea for Jobs Partnership was formed — to link churches that identify people who need jobs with businesses that will employ them.

Jobs Partnership consists of a 12-week program where potential employees learn practical job skills and biblical principles for the workplace. The curriculum is based on Pastor Tony Evans's Keys to Personal and Professional Success and includes prayer and a 45-minute lecture followed by a small-group discussion. The biweekly classes encompass "soft" skills such as attitudes, communication, integrity, conflict resolution, and stewardship, and "hard" skills such as résumé writing, interviewing, and getting a job. The program ends with a formal graduation.

Jobs Partnership is dependent on urban and suburban churches and business partners working together. The students are embedded in a web of support from the classroom to the workplace, minimizing the risk for potential employers. Applicants to Jobs Partnership must meet with pastors and be sponsored by churches in their areas. Once admitted, they are assigned mentors, preferably from the sponsoring churches, who make at least two-year commitments. Employers who agree to hire graduates are expected to provide a job "buddy" for each student and to report graduates' progress back to the sponsoring church. Suburban church partners covenant to refer business partners and job mentors to Jobs Partnership and to assist with other specific needs.

Jobs Partnership of Raleigh has received national attention based on its demonstrated success in mobilizing churches and the business community to assist welfare recipients. Mangum, the CEO of Jobs Partnership of Raleigh, was chosen by President Clinton to participate in the inauguration of the National Welfare to Work initiative. Jobs Partnership received the 1996 Business Award for the City of Raleigh. As of early 1999, the program has graduated 300 participants, 95 percent of whom have been successful in getting and keeping full-time jobs. One hundred church partners and more than 110 Raleigh business partners have joined. The program has been replicated in 28 cities, including Spartanburg, S.C.; Knoxville, Tenn.; Chattanooga, Tenn.; Oxford, N.C.; Washington, D.C.; Fresno, Calif.; Richmond, Va.; and Edenton, N.C. Similar programs are being developed in Peoria, Ill.; St. Louis, Mo.; Brenham, Texas; Baltimore, Md.; Dallas, Texas; Milwaukee, Wis.; Minneapolis, Minn.; Orlando, Fla.; Franklin, Tenn.; Denver, Colo.; and Colorado Springs, Colo.

Jobs Partnership has two training conferences a year in Raleigh. It will send interested churches information on its program and is happy to provide any church with help as needed.

THE EDUCATION AND EMPLOYMENT MINISTRY (TEEM)

Reverend Theo "Doc" Benson, Ministry Director
14 Northeast 13th Street
Oklahoma City, OK 73104
Phone: (405) 235-5671
Fax: (405) 235-5686
E-mail: staff@teem.org
Website: teem.org

Established February 15, 1987, by Theo "Doc" Benson, the son of a sharecropper, TEEM's mission is "to rebuild unemployed and underemployed individuals through a program of self-help so they can take responsibility for their lives." With a passion to see America's churches do a better job at helping the poor, Doc came to the inner city in 1981 to develop a program to help people help themselves. TEEM evolved as a three-part program that claims to spend less than $800 to move a person off welfare and into the workforce.

TEEM's approach to employing welfare recipients encompasses three programs. First is the Job Readiness Workshop, a five-day class that ends with a graduation ceremony, after which TEEM counselors will work with graduates for up to two years as they seek employment. TEEM professionals teach the job readiness classes, and professionals from the community provide various lectures throughout the week. Second, Transitional Employment Training is for those participants in the Job Readiness Workshop who aren't ready to get and keep jobs. These individuals are given temporary "bridge employment" that can last up to 90 days. "Bridge employment" consists of minimum-wage jobs and allows TEEM to work with participants on "job-keeping skills." Third, each person TEEM helps must attend a continuing education class at the facility. Course offerings include GED classes, AA meetings, computer literacy training, and literacy classes, all taught by community volunteers.

TEEM's success rate is impressive. More than 5,600 men and women have gone through the program, with more than 4,000 currently employed. Some 75 to 84 percent of TEEM graduates find and keep jobs. "Doc" welcomes the Christian community to learn from his ministry. The best approach, he says, is to spend two weeks at the program. TEEM will also send more specific information on the Job Readiness program to those who request it.

> "By Wednesday afternoon, something unusual is happening; the classroom full of widely varying people is becoming a close-knit, cohesive group of friends. The workshop isn't easy for anyone; it presents too many uncomfortable questions and forces participants to examine too many uncomfortable realities. ... On Thursday, the workshop participants leave the classroom one-by-one to go upstairs to the interview studio. ... 'If I made it through that, I can get through a real interview,' says Judy. 'It can't be any worse.' ...
>
> "At the end of the week, [Daryl] cites that bit of encouragement as one of the things that made him feel better about himself and his future. 'I feel like I can do anything,' he says."
>
> Roy Maynard, "Oklahoma City's TEEM: Building a Bridge to Employment," *Philanthropy, Culture and Society,* June 1997.

THE WASHINGTON PROJECT

Sharon Ricks, Executive Director
4025 9th Street, SE
Washington, DC 20032
Phone: (202) 561-5112
Fax: (202) 561-1004
E-mail: sricks@oncon.com

In 1997, leaders from urban and suburban churches in the Washington, D.C., area had a vision to start a collaborative economic development ministry. The Washington Project formally started in July 1998 to deliver the tools and support needed to Washington, D.C., residents desiring to start their own small or home-based businesses. They now have several churches on the board and widespread community support.

The ministry is open to grassroots entrepreneurs, provided they enjoy hard work and have a positive attitude. It is divided into two phases. First, during the 12-week "Entrepreneurial Study Program," students (called "peer learners") assess their aptitude for self-employment and the possibilities for their business ideas. They are partnered with a volunteer coach who assists them in developing their business plans. Second, during the "Micro-Business Laboratory Program," graduates from phase one are partnered with business-experienced mentors, who meet with them for at least six months. During this phase, the business plans are finalized, and seminars and workshops on such topics as money management are offered. Some of these classes are prerequisites for those seeking a start-up loan from The Washington Project. Loans are given up to $1,000 and are dependent on income.

> "Through the Washington Project, low-income people have the opportunity to get business training, credit and ongoing technical assistance so that they can start their own businesses. Trainers and mentors cover principles with clients such as bookkeeping, taxes, marketing, pricing and business start-up issues such as licensing."
>
> From the Washington Project brochure.

Though still relatively new, this idea looks promising. Eleven people graduated December 19, 1998, from the "Entrepreneurial Study Program" and are now in the "Micro-Business Laboratory Program." While the ministry is open to anyone, several members of the first class are among the "working poor" or living below the poverty line. The Washington Project will send interested churches and business leaders basic information. Staffers are currently developing a training manual so that their approach can be replicated in other areas.

WINGS

The Community Outreach Center
Kevin Bradley, CEO and Founder of the Outreach Foundation
816 S. Main Street
Bel Air, MD 21014
Phone: (410) 838-2353
Fax: (410) 838-6896
E-mail: kbradley5@compuserve.com

Founded in 1992 by a former stockbroker, the Community Outreach Center has developed a successful, biblically based approach called WINGS to move welfare recipients into jobs. WINGS is a 40-hour training seminar, taught over the course of one week, that teaches welfare recipients initiative, self-sufficiency, and job readiness skills. It is designed much like a middle- to upper-management training seminar. WINGS believes that "job placement is an event, not a process." Its main focus is moving motivated, passionate people back into the workforce.

The WINGS one-week seminar utilizes corporate trainers to teach the classes. Training topics include managing change, personal time management, communication skills, setting goals, establishing a personal vision plan, resource management for financial security, interview skills, customer service, building teamwork, stress management, and a personal style inventory (an MBTI-like instrument). CEOs, Human Resource Directors, and Temporary Agency Directors are invited to the class to observe participants and to recruit them after their graduation. This approach decreases the amount of risk to the employer. All participants "graduate" at the end of the seminar and receive certificates of completion.

More than 73 percent of the 300 graduates of WINGS training are employed. This approach has been replicated in Orlando, Fla.; Chicago, Ill.; Washington, D.C.; Tacoma, Wash.; Tampa, Fla.; and Baltimore, Md. As of early 1999, training in eight additional cities is underway. The Outreach Foundation provides training materials, trainers, and technical support to churches that want to adopt its approach.

> "I had come to the conclusion that welfare was a way of life for me and my family. But now I see how a job can change the entire way I look at my life."
>
> Tanya Riddle (WINGS Graduate), reprinted from WINGS brochure.

> "It is of no use to train someone and never give than an exit ramp out of poverty. ... Job placement is an event, not a process."
>
> Kevin Bradley, WINGS director

CLEARINGHOUSE MINISTRIES

Clearinghouse ministries — A clearinghouse is a community-wide hub for local churches to create databases of church volunteers and church ministries. Clearinghouses serve as bridges between social services and churches when social services have needs that pastors and laypeople can meet. They serve as protection mechanisms for churches from those who solicit many churches with the same request. They allow information-sharing within the Christian community and prevent churches from duplicating established ministries in their communities.

CORNERSTONE ASSISTANCE NETWORK
Mike Doyle, Executive Director
P.O. Box 820549
North Richland Hills, TX 76182
Phone: (817) 595-0274
Fax: (817) 595-0275
E-mail: mdoyle@azone.net
Website: www.canetwork.org

Founded in 1992, Cornerstone Assistance Network (CAN) developed from a pastor's vision for his church into a broad-based collaborative response to the poor in the community. CAN's goal is to assist and empower churches to use resources available in their communities. CAN does insist that each local church stay in control of its community outreach.

Locally, CAN works to equip local churches to meet the needs in the Tarrant County community. Since 1997, it has helped more than 20,000 people in its community through the many church volunteers in its network and a full-time staff of 15. CORE Net is CAN's computerized network of volunteers and resources from the 125 churches that have accessed one or more of Cornerstone's programs. CORE Net identifies church volunteers who are able to meet ministry needs in the community.

CAN provides training and technical assistance for churches across the country. This includes conducting an inventory of the gifts within the church body and one day of training on why the church should be involved in outreach and what the church wants to do. CAN also provides ongoing support services for churches in its area. CAN is happy to share information and advice on starting a like ministry. It has been conceptually replicated in Oklahoma City, Oklahoma,[106] and Tulsa, Oklahoma.[107] Each ministry is independently owned and operated.

LOVE INC (IN THE NAME OF CHRIST)

In partnership with World Vision USA
Pattie Juarez, Love INC Coordinator
P.O. Box 9716, Mail Stop 312
Federal Way, WA 98063-9716
Phone: (800) 777-5277   Fax: (253) 815-3341
E-mail: pjuarez@wvus.org
Website: www.worldvision.org/worldvision/wvususfo.nsf/stable/usfo or
www.surf-ici.com/pk/love_inc.htm[108]

Founded in 1976 by Virgil Gulker and adopted by World Vision in 1988, Love INC stands for Love In the Name of Christ. It is a community-wide clearinghouse for area churches to link laypeople with their neighbors in need. Every Love INC affiliate operates on the same model: The local affiliate receives a request for individual assistance and then links each request with the nearest church that has agreed to provide assistance when asked. Each Love INC affiliate has a databank of church volunteers, specifically stating what each layperson is able to do to assist someone. Each affiliate may also manage in-kind goods that are provided by participating churches. Referrals to Love INC come from the participating churches and social service agencies in the community. Love INC serves as a screen for referrals and helps prevent individuals in need from going from church to church with the same needs.

As of February 1999, there are 100 Love INC affiliates in 36 states. Five thousand churches and 71,000 church volunteers are involved nationally. In 1997, approximately 150,000 needs were met through 3,528 participating churches. In 1998, those figures had grown to more than 160,000 needs and 4,448 participating churches. Each affiliate is locally owned and operated. Love INC will send interested individuals and churches videos and preliminary information on how to get started.

Chapter Nine

SERVICE TRIPS IN THE UNITED STATES

W e recommend that churches use service trips to expose their youth groups, adult Sunday School groups, or other groups to the needs of a low-income neighborhood with the goal of developing a continuous relationship with one or two churches there. Additionally, it is highly recommended that a suburban church partner with an existing ministry and established leader in the low-income neighborhood in planning this type of service trip. Eventually, these trips should evolve into reciprocal relationships with particular churches or neighborhoods and should provide opportunities for those in the low-income community to serve the visiting church in its neighborhood in some capacity.

The following Christian organizations sponsor service trips to low-income communities in the United States. Leaders of these ministries are dedicated to unifying the body of Christ across class, race, and region. These ministries are designed to challenge, equip, and strengthen Christians in the United States for a fuller commitment to serve our country's neediest. Some service trips are day or weekend trips; others are as long as summer mission trips or two-year internships. Many trips are designed specifically for suburban church members, from junior-high age on up.

ADVENTURES IN MISSIONS

6000 Wellspring Trail
Gainesville, GA 30506
Phone: (770) 983-1060
Fax: (770) 983-1061
E-mail: AIM_Gainesville@juno.com

Adventures in Missions (AIM), headed by Seth Barnes, is an interdenominational missions organization that provides a variety of short-term projects for church groups and individuals, both overseas and in America. This unique organization tailors its projects to fit youth group ministry skills. Summer trips include inner-city and rural ministry as well as ministries among Native Americans. AIM also has spring break projects in many of the same places as its summer trips, and offers many service opportunities for adults.

CAMPUS CRUSADE FOR CHRIST

Here's Life Inner City
130 West 44th Street
New York, NY 10036
Phone: (212) 382-2838
Fax: (212) 921-9406
Website: www.urbanlink.com

Campus Crusade for Christ provides many opportunities to learn about urban ministry. College-age students may apply to be a part of "Summer in the City," which brings students together for an orientation and training week, then splits them into teams to minister at various sites around cities. Campus Crusade for Christ also offers an "Urban Immersion" experience for groups of college students during spring break. This five-day vision trip will acquaint college students with the organization's work in the city. In addition, Campus Crusade for Christ encourages families and church groups to learn more about ministry in the city by participating in "Vision Tours" at their various ministry sites.

THE CENTER FOR STUDENT MISSIONS

27302 Calle Arroyo
San Juan Capistrano, CA 92675
Phone: (714) 248-8200
Fax: (714) 248-7753
E-mail: csmhq@ix.netcom.com
Website: www.csm.org

The Center for Student Missions (CSM), headed by Noel Becchetti, brings students and adults of all ages into the inner city for ministry. Instead of creating its own projects, CSM links with existing churches and agencies to help them with their ministries. It serves groups from around the country by tailoring urban mission experiences that range in length from single weekends to 10 days. CSM books church groups year-round to minister in Los Angeles; Chicago; Washington, D.C.; Houston; and Toronto. The staff of the Center for Student Missions assists youth groups at every stage of the process, from helping alleviate parental fears to helping youth understand what they are learning once they are in the city. Students may minister in shelters, missions, children's programs, clubs, churches, parks, residential hotels, food banks, soup kitchens, and neighborhood centers.

CONFRONTATION POINT MINISTRIES

P.O. Box 572
Crossville, TN 38557
Phone: (800) 884-8483
Fax: (931) 484-7819
E-mail: cpoint@upper-cumberland.net

Confrontation Point Ministries, headed by Randy Velker, has been combining the experiences of wilderness camping and servant outreach since 1980. This ministry accepts groups of all ages to participate in weeklong programs, customized to accomplish each group's goals. During the first part of the week, group members work together to serve the rural community surrounding Crossville, Tenn. Groups may serve in one of three projects. Through the home repair mission project, groups provide repair services for Appalachian families, assisting the elderly, the handicapped, and low-income families with basic housing needs. For the day-camp mission, group members lead activities for Appalachian children five to 10 years of age who are socially, economically, or emotionally deprived. Groups choosing to serve in the special need mission program will work in camp settings with the mentally challenged, the hearing impaired, or people with physical handicaps. At the end of the week, the group undertakes an adventure activity such as rock climbing, rafting or rappelling. The entire experience focuses on spiritual growth for the group, both individually and as a community.

EMMAUS MINISTRIES

921 W. Wilson
Chicago, IL 60640
Phone: (773) 334-6063
Fax: (773) 334-8638
E-mail: emmaus@ix.netcom.com
Web site: www.streets.org

Emmaus is an interdenominational Christian ministry located on the north side of Chicago. This ministry is dedicated to making Jesus known on the streets among the young adult men of Chicago's night community. Emmaus offers a unique opportunity for church groups, college classes, and other concerned Christians to interact with and learn from these people. It has designed "Immersion Nights" specifically to sensitize Christians to the reality and needs of this community, including the homeless, street kids, and people struggling with homosexuality. At the beginning of the night, Emmaus trains and informs participants about the area they will be visiting. Then male/female pairs are sent out onto the streets for three or four hours with the goals of building trust and learning from the people they meet, as well as helping with basic necessities. After their time on the street, the pairs meet as a group for a debriefing session. Through this short experience, individuals learn compassion and understanding for people on the street.

THE HOLLYWOOD URBAN PROJECT

City Dwellers
1760 N. Gower Street
Hollywood, CA 90028
Phone: (213) 463-9555
Fax: (213) 463-8127

The Hollywood Urban Project is a neighborhood organization, headed by Dan Hoffman, that ministers to the needs of south Hollywood, an economically impoverished area. Volunteers and interns care for families and form partnerships with existing community organizations. Through City Dwellers, the Project's 11-month urban internship program, Christian young adults between the ages of 21 and 29 share the hope and healing that are found in Christ with the people of this community. Interns go through three weeks of orientation, during which they learn about urban life and solutions to urban problems. They develop relationships with people in the community and participate in ongoing ministries, such as tutoring children or teaching English to adults. City Dwellers also provides opportunities for interns to learn from experts in community organizing and personal leadership and development. Interns live together in an environment where they share experiences and participate in times of group Bible study, worship, and guided reflection.

INTERNATIONAL TEAMS

U.S. Urban Ministry
2300 South Millard
Chicago, IL 60623
Phone: (773) 522-9636
Fax: (773) 522-9670
E-mail: itusurban@compuserve.com
Website: www.Iteams.org

Through International Teams' U.S. Urban Ministry, groups and individuals from around the country learn about and experience ministry in the inner city. International Teams helps interested groups interact with a wide variety of cultures in Philadelphia, Chicago, Boston, and Los Angeles. Groups spend weekends or whole weeks partnering with urban churches to help them with their needs. Urban Ministry internships and summer projects are also available for those willing to serve in the inner city for longer periods of time.

INTERNATIONAL UNION OF GOSPEL MISSIONS

1045 Swift
Kansas City, MO 64116
Phone: (816) 471-8023
Fax: (816) 471-3718
E-mail: iugm@iugm.org
Website: www.iugm.org

Since 1913, member ministries of the International Union of Gospel Missions have provided food, shelter, and numerous other services for the mentally ill, the elderly, the urban poor, and street youth. IUGM has many sites across the country at which individuals can participate in internships and short-term mission projects. Interested individuals may contact the IUGM headquarters to learn about available positions.

International Union Gospel Ministries has an excellent short-term urban mission directory at http://www.iugm.org/sumr-dir.html. The directory lists short-term opportunities in more than 50 cities in North America.

INTERVARSITY CHRISTIAN FELLOWSHIP

Urban Projects
264 N. Van Ness Avenue
Fresno, CA 93701
Phone/Fax: (209) 497-8739
E-mail: rwwhiteiam@aol.com
Website: www.gospelcom.net/iv

InterVarsity has urban projects located in 23 cities across the country. Coordinated by Randy White (see his book in Chapter Ten), they offer a wide variety of summer internships. Teams of interns spend six to eight weeks living in urban communities. During the day, students work with local churches and community ministries. In the evening, they have debriefing, Bible study, and worship. In addition to summer internships, InterVarsity offers one- to two-week immersion projects. During these brief "urban plunges," students visit local ministries, serve at one or more ministry sites, and learn about opportunities for further training and service. Both types of short-term trips are intended to provide intensive exposure to the city. Through InterVarsity's Urban Projects, students learn about inner-city ministry from established urban leaders and wrestle with issues such as poverty, justice, and racial reconciliation.

JOHN M. PERKINS FOUNDATION FOR RECONCILIATION AND DEVELOPMENT

1909 Robinson Street
Jackson, MS 39209
Phone: (601) 354-1563
Fax: (601) 352-6882
E-mail: jmpfoffice@aol.com

John Perkins is continuing the work of his son Spencer, who passed away in January 1998. In Spencer's memory, a recreational park and retreat center is being built as a youth training center for leadership and racial reconciliation, with a major focus on raising up leadership in the neighborhood. Groups who share the vision of partnership and local leadership development are invited to spend a week in Jackson helping to build this center with other dedicated individuals of the John M. Perkins Foundation. (See Chapter Ten for more on John Perkins and the John M. Perkins Foundation.)

KIDS ACROSS AMERICA

The I'm Third Foundation
1429 Lakeshore Drive
Branson, MO 65616
Phone: (417) 335-8400
Fax: (417) 335-8473

Kids Across America, an extension of Camp Kanakuk-Kanakomo, ministers among urban young people. Every summer, young urban men and women from all over the country meet and create friendships in a camp setting. Here, students grow in their understanding of the Gospel through daily Bible studies, small group sharing, and one-on-one counseling. During Kids Across America Camps, young people participate in a wide variety of sports and adventure activ-

ities. The camps are staffed by athletes from numerous American colleges.

LAMBS CHURCH OF THE NAZARENE

130 West 44th Street
New York, NY 10036
Phone: (212) 575-0300
Fax: (212) 768-1380
E-mail: tgrant@ccci.org

Lambs Church of the Nazarene, located in New York City's famous Times Square, offers numerous experiences for individuals and groups of all ages. Under the leadership of Youth Pastor Troy Grant, youth groups participate in a three-day "Urban Plunge" or a weeklong "Urban Immersion." The goal of these projects is for youth to see New York City through God's eyes. Youth serve the needy by working in soup kitchens, distributing clothing and blankets, doing street evangelism, and much more. Students may also commit to the church's summer-long internship program. Interns work in children's, youth, or adult ministries. Adults can participate in "Work and Witness" groups, where they use their skills to provide needed services. Families are also welcome to spend their vacations at Lambs Church of the Nazarene. Space is limited, but the cost is moderate by New York City standards.

METRO MINISTRIES INTERNATIONAL

P.O. Box 695
Brooklyn, NY 11237
Phone: (718) 453-3352
Fax: (718) 453-7177
E-mail: metrossny@aol.com
Website: www.metroministries.com

Metro Ministries International is an inner-city children's ministry based in

Brooklyn, New York. Under the leadership of founder Bill Wilson, Metro reaches 20,000 children a week through its "Saturday Sunday School" and "Sidewalk Sunday School" programs. Tuesday through Friday, staff and volunteers conduct after-school "Sidewalk Sunday School" at 30 different sites around the city. Tuesday evenings, they reach 800 teenagers through their "Club Life" youth program. Metro Ministries also reaches the children's families through visitation and family Sunday worship services. Groups and individuals may schedule short Saturday trips or plan to spend a week participating in the work of the ministry. Six-month internships are also available. Interested callers should ask for the Guest Relations Department.

MISSION YEAR

c/o Kingdomworks
P.O. Box 12589
Philadelphia, PA 19151
Phone: (610) 645-0800
Fax: (610) 645-0802
E-mail: kworks@juno.com

Mission Year, led by Bart Campolo, is a one-year ministry program that places teams of six or seven young adults as missionaries in inner-city communities. Each volunteer becomes part of a solid local church, works at a community service job, and participates in neighborhood outreach in order to develop relationships with neighbors and share the love of God. Volunteers raise a majority of their own support. Mission Year is a program of Kingdomworks and currently operates in Oakland and Philadelphia.

Dave Thompson, former missionary with Mission Year, with his friends in Philadelphia.

MOUNTAIN T.O.P.

2704 12th Avenue, South
Nashville, TN 37211
Phone: (615) 298-1575
E-mail: OntheMTOP@aol.com

Mountain T.O.P. (Tennessee Outreach Project) is an interdenominational Christian mission affiliated with the Tennessee Conference of the United Methodist Church. This ministry equips students and adults to meet the physical, spiritual, social, and emotional needs of Tennessee Cumberland Mountain families. Through worship, reading, reflection, and small-group activities, groups are prepared to participate in week-long service projects consisting of home repairs and/or day camp ministry to children in the community. College students may participate in "Break Out," a spring break outreach program.

THE PITTSBURGH PROJECT

2801 North Charles Street
Pittsburgh, PA 15214
Phone: (412) 321-1678
Fax: (412) 321-3813
E-mail: pghproject@aol.com

The Pittsburgh Project, led by Saleem Ghubril, is an urban, neighborhood-based Christian community development organization. During its week-long summer service camps, middle and high school students provide home repair to the city's needy residents. Evenings are spent in worship, singing, recreation and discussion in large- and small-group settings. The Pittsburgh Project's goal is to inspire servant mindsets in students.

REACH OUT MINISTRIES

Contact: Tim Brown
Suite 201
Norcross, GA 30092
Phone: (770) 441-2247
Fax: (770) 449-7544
Website: www.reach-out.org

Reach Out Ministries, founded by youth speaker and author Barry St. Clair, offers a variety of resources to equip youth for ministry. Through domestic summer mission trips, students learn to serve others in a variety of capacities. Projects range from spending a week in Miami ministering to youth and learning cross-cultural ministry, to teaching Vacation Bible School to inner-city children in Atlanta, to cleaning houses and building relationships with disabled senior adults. Students are also exposed to the plight of the homeless.

URBAN HANDS

755 Eighth Street, NW
Washington, DC 20001
Phone: (202) 347-8355
Fax: (202) 347-6360

Urban HANDS (Helping Another in Need by Demonstrating Servanthood), headed by Paget Rhee and Jennifer Mitroff, is a year-round program located at Calvary Baptist Church in the heart of Washington, D.C. This weeklong program is designed to bring church groups face-to-face with homelessness and poverty. During the first phase of their stay in D.C., individuals participate in "Poverty Simulation." For 24 hours, students are asked to give up their possessions, money, and normal ways of life. The simulation is designed to help students gain a greater understanding of the circumstances that complicate the situations of homeless people. The second phase of Urban Hands places youth at many different work sites throughout the city. At the end of each day, groups meet to discuss and process what they have learned. All groups stay at the church (which, incidentally, is located next door to Family Research Council's Washington, D.C., headquarters).

VOICE OF CALVARY MINISTRIES

1655 St. Charles Street
Jackson, MS 39209
Phone: (601) 353-1635
Fax: (601) 944-0403

John Perkins founded Voice of Calvary Ministries in the early 1960s. (See Chapter Ten for more information on John Perkins.) The 26 staff members and more than 600 volunteers are committed to the goal of "individual empowerment and community development, helping people gain greater access to the American economic system." Volunteer groups are invited to participate in one-week housing development work projects. Individuals and groups may also participate in an eight-week summer internship program that focuses on health care, teaching, photography and writing, and volunteer leadership. Voice of Calvary provides training for participating groups in Christian community development with a focus on reconciliation (with God and one's fellow man), relocation (moving to a low-income community as a way to serve God and one's fellow man) and redistribution (stewardship of one's resources for the empowerment of others).

WORLD CHANGERS

North American Mission Board
of the Southern Baptist Convention
4200 North Point Parkway
Alpharetta, GA 30022-4176
Phone: (800) 462-VOLS or
(770) 410-6000
Fax: (770) 410-6014
Website: www.studentz.com/mobilize

The North American Mission Board of the Southern Baptist Convention provides opportunities for groups, individual adults, and students in junior high through college to minister among the needy in communities across America. Through World Changers, groups and individuals partner with community agencies, church associations, state conventions, ministry centers, and local churches to meet the housing needs of communities. Projects take place in cities and rural areas across America. They range from light to heavy construction and are combined with worship activities.

WORLD IMPACT

2001 South Vermont Avenue
Los Angeles, CA 90007
Phone: (213) 735-1137
Fax: (213) 735-2576
E-mail: info@worldimpact.org

World Impact, led by Dr. Keith Phillips, incarnationally ministers to inner-city communities through church planting and the development of ministries around local concerns. Through relationships, the organization disciples and equips neighborhood residents to lead the church in the city. World Impact's summer intern program, "Urban Serve," is active in 12 cities across the United States. Lasting eight to 10 weeks, it is designed to give college-age students the opportunity to serve alongside World Impact missionaries. Students minister in urban, camp, school, or medical clinic settings.

WORLD SERVANTS

7130 Portland Avenue South
Richfield, MN 55423-3264
Phone: (612) 866-0010
Fax: (612) 866-0078
E-mail:
 TGibson@worldservants.org
Website: www.worldservants.org

World Servants, led by Tim Gibson, provides mission projects for teens, families and adults in the United States as well as abroad. In North America, a team may spend a week ministering in a rural location, such as the Appalachian Mountains of Kentucky or West Virginia.

YOUNG LIFE

Contact: Mike O'Leary
P.O. Box 520
Colorado Springs, CO 80901-0520
Phone: (719) 381-1800
Fax: (719) 381-1755

Young Life, an international outreach to middle and high school students, has a two-year internship program for adults interested in full-time, relational youth ministry. During this internship, individuals receive theological training at accredited seminaries. In addition, they receive hands-on ministry experience with youth in a broad variety of social, economic and multicultural communities. Over 300 interns are located in cities and towns across the United States, including Philadelphia, New York, Boston, Pittsburgh, Baltimore, and Washington, D.C.

YOUTH FOR CHRIST

Serving USA
P.O. Box 228822
Denver, CO 80222
Phone: (888) SERVIN-1
Fax: (303) 843-6793
E-mail: MTreves@aol.com
Website: www.yfc.org/worldoutreach

Youth for Christ, a national ministry to middle and high school students, has a weeklong summer mission project that builds students' vision for outreach. During the summer, 1,200 students meet in Indianapolis to serve at one of 75 various work sites in the Indianapolis area. The students are housed in tents at a local fairgrounds. During the day, they work at their designated sites; in the evening, they meet back at the fairgrounds for worship and biblical teaching. Future plans include the ministry's expanding its location to five other cities across the United States.

YOUTH WORKS

P.O. Box 8589
Minneapolis, MN 55408
Phone: (800) 968-8504 or
(612) 729-5444
Fax: (612) 729-4113
E-mail: youthworks@aol.com

Youth Works, headed by Paul Bertolson, organizes domestic mission trips tailored to the needs of junior high and high school students.   Its urban projects, located in Colorado, Tennessee, and Minnesota, give students the opportunity to serve others by doing home repairs and working at homeless shelters.   Youth Works also enables youth to minister in various rural areas, such as Indian reservations in Montana, Wyoming, South Dakota, and Arizona; the shrimping areas of Alabama; and the mountains of West Virginia.   At the rural sites, students work on low-maintenance housing repairs and minister to area children through Vacation Bible School programs.

"I consistently find that those churches that respond most compassionately to the needy are those that have sent out from their own congregations people to live and walk and eat and breathe among the poor, and who have then heard their eyewitness accounts of the need, the opportunity, and the challenge. ...[As a short-term missionary among the poor] you can bring your new understanding and vision back to your home church and help them to shape a meaningful Christian response to the cries of the needy."

John M. Perkins, *Beyond Charity* (Grand Rapids: Baker Books, 1993), p. 167.

Chapter Ten

ADDITIONAL RESOURCES FOR YOUR CHURCH

SUGGESTED READING

Acting on Your Faith: Congregations Making a Difference — A Guide to Success in Service and Social Action
by Victor N. Claman and David E. Butler with Jessica A. Boyatt (Boston: Insights, 1994), (800) 323-6809
The book's 100 stories and 250 photos show how congregations from 14 faiths and denominations have made a difference in their communities. This is a great book for highlighting possibilities for a congregation.

The American City and the Evangelical Church: A Historical Overview
by Harvie M. Conn (Grand Rapids: Baker Books, 1994), (800) 877-2665
Missiologist and Westminister Seminary Professor Harvie M. Conn presents an historical survey to articulate why a dichotomy exists between American cities and the evangelical church. This book is recommended for pastors and lay leaders interested in evangelical church history, particularly from the 1920s to the present.

Basic Steps Toward Community Ministry
by Carl Dudley (Washington, D.C.: The Alban Institute, 1991), (202) 244-7320.
Dudley, professor of church and community at Hartford Seminary, draws insights on church-based ministry from case studies of 32 Illinois and Indiana churches. This provides a good guide for churches for defining their parish and identifying the strengths and limits of their congregation.

Building Communities from the Inside Out: A Path Toward Finding and Mobilizing a Community's Assets
by John L. McKnight and John P. Kretzmann (Chicago: ACTA Publications, 1993), (800) 397-2282.
This very practical 376-page guidebook helps communities "map" and mobilize their assets, and team with others in their communities to improve their neighborhoods. Recommended for local community leaders, leaders of associations, business leaders, and church leaders who want to support effective, community-building strategies. Produced by the Neighborhood Innovations Network of Northwestern University.

Church Social Work: Helping the Whole Person in the Context of the Church
by Diana Garland (St. Davids, Pa.: North American Association of Christians in Social Work, 1992), (203) 270-8780.
Garland, a professional social worker, gives an introduction to church social work. This book is especially recommended for Christian social workers and for churches interested in hiring them to develop and lead their local ministry efforts.

Companion to the Poor
by Viv Grigg (Monrovia, Calif.: MARC, 1990), (800) 777-7752.
Grigg, adjunct professor at Fuller Theological Seminary and missionary in the squatter settlements of Manila, relates his autobiographical and theological reflections on ministry among the poor.

Congress and Civil Society: How Legislators Can Champion Civic Renewal in Their District
by April Lassiter (Washington, D.C.: The Heritage Foundation, 1998), (202) 546-4400.
This 51-page booklet explores how members of Congress are furthering the advance of private charities and grassroots problem-solving through non-legislative means. This is a good resource for established ministries desiring to gain recognition from their representatives or senators.

Cry of the Urban Poor
by Viv Grigg (Monrovia, Calif.: MARC, 1992), (800) 777-7752.
Grigg combines universal principles behind church planting among the poor with anthropological and sociological reflections. Both of Grigg's books are recommended for ministers and missionaries in low-income communities who are seeking Christian insight to inform their work.

Economic Empowerment Through the Church: A Blueprint for Community Development
by Gregory J. Reed (Grand Rapids: Zondervan, 1994), (800) 727-1309.
Written by an attorney, this is a practical how-to book for churches on the legal questions surrounding their community outreach programs. Topics include starting a church-based day care center and drug treatment center and starting a separate 501(c)(3) nonprofit to administer the church's outreach programs in the community.

Workbook and Supplemental Guide: Applying the Principles Found in The Welfare of My Neighbor.
by Amy Sherman; Deanna Carlson, editor. (Washington, D.C.: Family Research Council, 1999), (800)225-4008. Geared towards churches that want to increase their focus on relational ministries, this "how-to" supplement will guide them through basic steps to starting a mentoring ministry among welfare families. Helpful tools for assessing their church's current outreach ministries are included. Originally published by The Manhattan Institute, this supplement draws from the author's practical experience as the director of Urban Ministries at Trinity Presbyterian Church in Charlottesville, Va.

Helping a Neighbor in Crisis
Lisa Barnes Lampman, editor (Wheaton: Tyndale House Publishers, 1997), (800) 323-9400. More than 20 Christian community practitioners share wisdom, practical tips, and related Scripture on helping and encouraging a neighbor in a particular crisis. More than 30 crises are addressed, including domestic violence, substance abuse, children with special needs, and imprisonment of a family member. This book is designed to assist the layperson.

How to Mobilize Church Volunteers
by Marlene Wilson (Minneapolis: Augsburg Publishing House, 1997), (800) 328-4648. A practical, engaging book on increasing volunteerism in your church. Answers commonly asked questions about church volunteerism, including how the church can relate to community agencies, such as social services, that are seeking volunteers.

Journey to the Center of the City
by Randy White (Downers Grove, Ill.: InterVarsity Press, 1996), (800) 843-7225. White, national director of Urban Projects for InterVarsity, tells how his family moved from a white suburban community into a low-income community to become neighbors of the poor. Designed for group discussions. Each chapter contains questions for reflection and discussion, and there is an appendix Bible study on God and the city.

Let's Get to Know Each Other: What White Christians Should Know About Black Christians
by Tony Evans (Nashville: Thomas Nelson, 1995), (800) 933-9673. Evans, pastor of Oak Cliff Bible Fellowship and president of the Urban Alternative in Dallas, details black heritage throughout the Bible and challenges black and white churches to unite to make a difference in America. He encourages black and white Christians to reconcile with one another and to learn to understand each other's culture and strengths.

Ministries of Mercy: The Call of the Jericho Road
by Timothy Keller (Phillipsburg, N.J.: P & R Publishing, 1997), (800) 631-0094. Keller, former director of Mercy Ministries for the Presbyterian Church of America, demonstrates that every Christian has the responsibility to help the needy. He outlines practical steps for mobilizing churches, families and individuals to Christ-like outreach. Relevant issues for churches, such as meeting needs within and outside the church, and ministering with limited resources, are addressed. A very good book for mission and local outreach pastors.

Spencer Perkins and Chris Rice share their personal story of Christian friendship at an InterVarsity conference.

More Than Equals: Racial Healing for the Sake of the Gospel
by Spencer Perkins and Chris Rice (Downers Grove, Ill.: InterVarsity Press, 1993), (800) 843-7225.
Perkins and Rice, best friends and partners in racial reconciliation, describe a decade of growth experienced through their black and white friendship, which lasted until Perkins's death in 1998. Their narrative provides a heartfelt challenge for racial reconciliation that extends into our personal relationships.

Next Steps in Community Ministry
by Carl Dudley (Washington, D.C.: The Alban Institute, 1996), (202) 244-7320.
This book is based on research and interviews with the 25 continuing church ministries from *Basic Steps Toward Community Ministry*. A practical book with summaries on motivation, organization, resources, and impact of church-based ministries.

No One Is Unemployable: Creative Solutions for Overcoming Barriers to Employment
by Debra L. Angel and Elisabeth E. Harney (Hacienda Heights, Calif.: WorkNet Publications, 1997), (888) 9-WORKNET.
Through their WorkNet model, Angel and Harney have demonstrated success in employing those deemed unemployable. In this practical handbook, the authors outline a range of realistic situations, barriers to obtaining employment, and step-by-step strategies to overcome these obstacles. This is a valuable resource for churches and employment agencies working with welfare recipients who have been labeled the "hardest to employ."

Books by Dr. John M. Perkins

These books are foundational for churches interested in developing and expanding their community outreach activities. They are all available through the Christian Community Development Association at (312) 762-0994. These are highly recommended for pastors, lay leaders, and church libraries.

Beyond Charity: The Call to Christian Community Development
by Dr. John M. Perkins (Grand Rapids: Baker Books, 1993).
Perkins details his vision for church outreach that moves beyond charity and handouts toward reconciliation and development.

He's My Brother
by Dr. John M. Perkins and Rev. Thomas A. Tarrants III (Grand Rapids: Chosen Books, 1994).
Perkins and Tarrants, a former Ku Klux Klan member who is now a pastor, present a personal account of reconciliation between races through their friendship.

Restoring At-Risk Communities: Doing It Together and Doing It Right

Dr. John M. Perkins, editor (Grand Rapids: Baker Books, 1995).

Perkins introduces the first-ever handbook for church-based Christian community development, written by 14 urban ministry professionals. A must read for churches.

Resurrecting Hope: Powerful Stories of How God Is Moving to Reach Our Cities

by Dr. John M. Perkins (Ventura, California: Regal Books, 1995).

An account of 12 churches that God is using to make a difference in their cities. New, innovative ideas, such as suburban and urban church partnerships, are presented for church ministry.

Real Hope in Chicago

by Wayne Gordon (Grand Rapids: Zondervan, 1995), (800) 727-1309.

Gordon, co-founder of the Christian Community Development Association and pastor of Lawndale Community Church, recounts the story of the rebirth of his decaying Chicago neighborhood. What began as a Bible study 25 years ago has turned into a multiracial neighborhood church with a staff of 150 that is evangelistic and socially committed. A truly inspiring book on relational Christian ministry in the inner city.

Reclaiming the Urban Family: How to Mobilize the Church as a Family Training Center

by Willie Richardson (Grand Rapids: Zondervan, 1996), (800) 727-1309.

Richardson, senior pastor of Christian Stronghold Baptist Church in Philadelphia, describes how his African-American church has become a Family Training Center that offers practical aid and biblical hope to families in the inner city. Resources for African-American family ministries are listed at the end of each chapter.

Restorers of Hope: Reaching the Poor in Your Community with Church-based Ministries that Work

by Amy L. Sherman (Wheaton: Crossway Books, 1997), (630) 682-4300.

This timely book describes and analyzes the work of several Christ-centered, church-based social welfare ministries. Describing why these ministries are working and giving practical advice for churches on increasing their outreach efforts, this is a must read for all churches desiring to advance their outreach work. Includes a detailed analysis of church and government partnerships, specifically within the context of welfare reform.

Servanthood: The Vocation of the Christian

by Darrow L. Miller (Scottsdale, Ariz.: Food for the Hungry, 1991), (602) 998-3100.

These 13 Bible studies on Christian servanthood were originally written for a group of Christian high school students from Ohio who were working with the poor in the Dominican Republic under the leadership of the international Christian ministry Food for the Hungry. Now available to the wider public, the 110-page workbook is a good tool for church groups, Bible study groups, and youth groups that want to explore biblical teaching on service through a well-organized Bible study.

Teaching Your Kids to Care: How to Discover and Develop the Spirit of Charity in Your Children

by Deborah Spaide (Secaucus, N.J.: Citadel Press, 1995), (800) 866-1966.

Written to assist parents in passing down charitable values to their children, this book describes 100 different charitable projects parents can initiate with their children, including adopting a needy family and starting a call-in program for latchkey kids. Designed for parents of children from kindergarten to high school.

A Time to Heal

by Stephen Berk (Grand Rapids: Baker Books, 1997), (800) 877-2665.

The life story of Dr. John Perkins, the esteemed Christian leader in the racial reconciliation movement and founder of the Christian Community Development Association. This is a must read for individuals who are interested in evangelical involvement in the civil rights movement and community development. It describes how one committed Christian man and his family have made a marked difference in America for the sake of the poor.

The Tragedy of American Compassion

by Marvin Olasky (Washington, D.C.: Regnery Publishing, 1992), (800) 462-6420.

Considered by many the most important book on welfare and social policy in a decade, this work makes the case for a return to private-sector compassionate efforts with an emphasis on one-on-one relationships, charity that demands work, and the importance of religion. A very detailed historical account of how Americans have responded to human need in times past and how human compassion has been mitigated by the growth of government welfare programs.

The Triumphs of Joseph

by Robert L. Woodson, Sr. (New York: The Free Press, 1998), (800) 223-2348.

Robert L. Woodson, Sr., president of the National Center for Neighborhood Enterprise, uses the biblical story of Joseph as a metaphor to emphasize the need to listen to and empower local leaders in community renewal efforts. He shows that the leadership necessary for community change already exists in the inner city and the streets of America, and that we must find, encourage and support these "Josephs."

Winning the Race to Unity

by Clarence Shuler (Chicago: Moody Press, 1998), (800) 678-8812.

Packed with experience from more than 30 years of cross-cultural ministry, this book by the former director of Black Pastor Ministries at Focus on the Family offers insights to help predominantly white Christian organizations and churches minister among minorities and improve race relations.

A World Without Welfare

(Washington, D.C.: Family Research Council, 1997), (800) 225-4008.

In 1995, just prior to the passage of the monumental welfare reform law, the Family Research Council convened a symposium of public policy experts and ministry directors to examine the role of welfare in society and where it might be leading.

HELPFUL NEWSLETTERS

Into Action

Leadership Training Network
2501 Cedar Springs LB-5, Suite 200
Dallas, TX 75201
Phone: (800) 765-5323 or
(214) 969-5950
Fax: (214) 969-9392
E-mail: BradSmith1@compuserve.com
Website: www.leadnet.org
Published quarterly by the
Leadership Network
Complimentary

Into Action, a national Christian newsletter on lay ministry, features church profiles, new resources, and key trends in team ministry and lay ministry efforts.

Philanthropy, Culture, and Society

Capital Research Center
1513 16th Street, NW
Washington, DC 20036
Phone: (202) 483-6900
Fax: (202) 483-6902
E-mail: crc@capitalresearch.org
Website: www.capitalresearch.org/crc/pcs
Published monthly by the
Capital Research Center
Subscription: $30/year (past issues are available on the web site)

Philanthropy, Culture and Society, a conservative policy newsletter, examines in detail the successes and failures of lesser-known charities that are assisting the poor creatively and compassionately.

Urban Perspectives ...reflections on faith, grace and the city

FCS Urban Ministries, Inc.
750 Glenwood Avenue, SE
P.O. Box 17628
Atlanta, GA 30316
Phone: (404) 627-4304
Fax: (404) 624-5299
E-mail: fcslupton@aol.com
Website: www.ccda.org/fcs/
(also available online)
Distributed monthly by FCS
Urban Ministries, Inc.
Complimentary

Urban Perspectives, a two-page newsletter, is a collection of anecdotes and first-person reflections on life in the inner city. Robert D. Lupton, the author and president of FCS Urban Ministries, gives glimpses into the life of a Christian family that has purposely lived and ministered among the poor for years.

CHRISTIAN MINISTRIES THAT SUPPORT CHURCH-BASED OUTREACH TO THE POOR

CENTER FOR URBAN RESOURCES

990 Buttonwood Street, 6th Floor
Philadelphia, PA 19123
Phone: (215) 386-8242
Fax: (215) 386-8248
E-mail: cur@libertynet.org
Website: www.libertynet.org/cur

Founded in 1987 by Dr. Willie Richardson, pastor of Christian Stronghold Baptist Church, the Center for Urban Resources helps urban churches obtain the necessary resources to transform individuals, families, and whole communities through the vehicle of the church. CUR's mission is to be a bridge between these churches and other resources so that strengths are shared for maximum community impact. CUR provides technical assistance to help developing nonprofit organizations in such areas as tax-exempt status, board development, strategy planning, budgeting essentials, and other pertinent issues. The objective of its Community Impact Institute is to provide training and practical and technical assistance to churches in the areas of organizational and resource development, teaching them how to better access human and financial resources for the support of needed community service programs they offer. CUR also publishes a directory of community service programs that is updated and distributed annually, as well as providing consulting services to other cities.

CHRISTIAN COMMUNITY DEVELOPMENT ASSOCIATION

3827 W. Ogden Avenue
Chicago, IL 60623
Phone: (773) 762-0994
Fax: (773) 762-5772
E-mail: chiccda@aol.com
Website: www.ccda.org/

Founded in 1989 by Dr. John M. Perkins and the John M. Perkins Foundation for Reconciliation and Development, CCDA is a national association of more than 400 churches and ministries and 3,000 individuals, in 35 states and more than 100 cities. CCDA's purpose is to develop a strong fellowship of those involved in Christian community development, to support and encourage existing Christian community development efforts, and to help establish new Christian community development efforts. CCDA works with Christian community development ministries to mobilize spiritual and physical resources through the church in a community-determined way.

CCDA holds an annual national winter conference that offers hundreds of practical seminars led by some of the best ministry practitioners in the country. CCDA's membership directory is a useful guide to its more than 400 member organizations. Many of its practitioners are available for consulting and speaking at churches and conferences.

COMPASSION INTERNATIONAL, US CHILDSHARE

3955 Craigwood Drive
Colorado Springs, CO 80997
Phone: (800) 334-KIDS
Fax: (719) 594-6271
E-mail: USAInfo@us.ci.org
Website: www.ci.org/HELP/usa.htm

Founded in 1992, Compassion US ChildShare is Compassion International's ministry to children in need in the United States. Rather than financially supporting one child overseas as with Compassion International's program, a US ChildShare partner supports one church-based ministry in America that serves at-risk children, usually in the inner city or on a Native American reservation. US ChildShare partners receive descriptions and photographs of the specific outreach centers they are helping and regular updates on the ministry. US ChildShare sponsorship starts at $20/month.

Compassion US ChildShare has produced an introductory 12-minute video on children's needs in America, titled *Our Country, Our Children, Our Future*. This describes its program as well as highlighting why church-based ministry among low-income communities is vital to the future of our country.

COUNCIL OF LEADERSHIP FOUNDATIONS

Reid Carpenter, Chair of Council of Leadership Foundations and Executive Director, Pittsburgh Leadership Foundation
100 Ross Street, 4th Floor
Pittsburgh, PA 15219
Phone: (412) 281-3752
Fax: (412) 281-2312
E-mail: carpenter@plf.org
Website: www.plf.org

Started in 1994 by the Pittsburgh Leadership Foundation, the Council of Leadership Foundations (CLF) is a national urban network for qualifying leadership foundations. The shared mission of the Council of Leadership Foundations and its member leadership foundations is to aid and equip united Christian leadership and to show Christ's generosity among the poor. Each leadership foundation functions as an extensive ministry hub, developer, mobilizer, and educator for an urban geographic area. The foundations all provide practical leadership to city leaders and are dedicated to the well-being of the citizens of their respective communities, including personal redemption through Jesus Christ and community reformation. The first leadership foundation, the Pittsburgh Leadership Foundation, has more than 20 years of organized experience in citywide Christian community development.

Applicants for CLF membership must show a broad base of collaboration with and support from the city and its churches; a plan of action derived from careful assessment of that city's needs; and a viable vision for extending their capacity for effective service. The Council includes groups in more than 20 cities, including Chicago, Minneapolis, New York, Philadelphia, Pittsburgh and Seattle.

HABITAT FOR HUMANITY INTERNATIONAL

121 Habitat Street
Americus, GA 31709
Phone: (912) 924-6935
Fax: (912) 924-6541
E-mail: public_info@habitat.org,
 Church_Relations@habitat.org
Website: www.habitat.org

Founded in 1976 by Millard Fuller, Habitat for Humanity is a Christian ministry employing the "theology of the hammer," where people from all walks of life come together to build houses for and with God's people in need. Churches are the primary partners in Habitat's work to end homelessness through building affordable homes for low-income families. In 1996, more than 24,000 churches partnered with Habitat affiliates in some way, including contributing millions of hours of labor to erect homes. Habitat projects are a wonderful way for churches to build relationships with other churches, community activists, and low-income families.

INNERCHANGE

Church Resource Ministries
1240 N. Lakeview Ave. #120
Anaheim, CA 92807-1831
Phone: (714) 779-0370
Fax: (714) 779-0189
E-mail: crm@crmnet.org
Website: www.crmnet.org

InnerCHANGE is a Christian order composed of communities of missionaries who live and minister among the poor, primarily in the United States. The idea was birthed in 1983 as a means to minister "inside out" — to live and work among the poor, rather than driving in and doing service on the weekends. InnerCHANGE missionaries proclaim the kingdom of God one neighborhood at a time through the raising up of leaders for church planting, church renewal, and community transformation. Now with more than 30 staff members, InnerCHANGE communities live among major people groups in five cities: Santa Ana, California; Los Angeles; San Francisco; Minneapolis; and Phnom Penh, Cambodia. InnerCHANGE is a division of Church Resource Ministries in Anaheim, California.

INTERNATIONAL UNION OF GOSPEL MISSIONS

1045 Swift Street
Kansas City, MO 64116-4127
Phone: (800) 624-5156
Fax: (816) 471-3718
E-mail: iugm@iugm.org
Website: www.iugm.org

Founded in 1913, the International Union of Gospel Missions (IUGM) is an association of organizations and individuals involved in rescue ministry. The purpose of the association is to develop programs that advance the cause of Jesus Christ; promote cooperation; build fellowship; provide services to local ministries; establish new rescue ministries; maintain national contact among churches, other evangelical outreaches, and governmental and secular social service organizations; and provide education and training. There are more than 250 rescue missions across the United States, primarily located in inner cities. IUGM-member rescue missions provide emergency food and shelter, youth and family services, rehabilitation programs for the addicted, and assistance to the elderly poor and at-risk youth.

In 1996, IUGM rescue missions served more than 30 million meals, provided 12 million nights of lodging, distributed more than 24 million pieces of clothing, and graduated more than 20,000 homeless men and women into productive living. IUGM rescue

missions encourage area churches to support their ministry as they share in the common biblical cause of assisting the poor.

INTERNATIONAL URBAN ASSOCIATES

5151 N. Clark Street, 2nd Floor
Chicago, IL 60640
Phone: (773) 275-9260
Fax: (773) 275-9969
E-mail: iuai@ais.net

Formed in 1989 by urban missiologist Ray Bakke, International Urban Associates (IUA) educates and motivates the body of Christ to fulfill the church's mission to take the healing and transforming power of the gospel into the world's cities. IUA works with associates, partnerships, and networks to aid the cause of international urban missions. In the United States, IUA has partnered with several national urban networks to pioneer a creative urban church agenda. IUA develops and facilitates city consultations where leaders of various churches and Christian organizations come together to address the issues that are important to specific cities. Additionally, the IUA Associates Network is a worldwide network of expert practitioners and theologians of urban ministry in major cities worldwide.

JOHN M. PERKINS FOUNDATION FOR RECONCILIATION AND DEVELOPMENT

1909 Robinson St.
Jackson, MS 39209
Phone: (601) 354-1563
Fax: (601) 352-6882
E-mail: jmpfoffice@aol.com

Founded by John M. Perkins, this foundation's mission is to develop leaders and resources to further the vision of holistic Christian community development and racial reconciliation. This ministry is rooted in an authentic demonstration of racial reconciliation and church-based community development, and offers resources such as books and videos. It also holds national Christian community development workshops and consultations on the biblical principles of Christian community development and racial reconciliation. In addition, the foundation helped to found, and currently supports, the Christian Community Development Association (CCDA).

The Perkins Foundation has recently launched new ministry efforts in Jackson, Miss., including the continuation of some aspects that were formerly part of Reconcilers Fellowship. For more information on these endeavors, contact the Perkins Foundation office.

LEADERSHIP TRAINING NETWORK

2501 Cedar Springs Road, Suite 200
Dallas, TX 75201
Phone: (800) 765-5323
Fax: (214) 969-9392
Website: www.leadnet.org/c9ltnpage.html

Leadership Training Network (LTN) helps churches mobilize the laity to serve. LTN provides the following helpful products and training resources to churches: (1) *Into Action*, a quarterly newsletter featuring church profiles, new resources, and key trends in team ministry; (2) Leadership Training Networks, interactive one- and two-day seminars for church leadership teams on ministry development and expansion; (3) Church Consultant Workshops, five-day "hands on" workshops for churches desiring to implement lay mobilization movements; and (4) The Starter Kit for Mobilizing Ministry, a manual for churches developing lay ministry. Leadership Training Network is a division of the Leadership Network in Dallas, Texas.

THE SALVATION ARMY USA

Commissioner Robert A. Watson,
National Commander
P.O. Box 269
Alexandria, VA 22313
Phone: (703) 684-5500
Fax: (703) 684-3478
Website: www.salvationarmyusa.org

Founded by William Booth in 1865, the Salvation Army began as an evangelistic ministry to the outcasts of society in the slums of London, including the poor, thieves, prostitutes, gamblers, and drunkards. The goal was to lead them to Christ and then to link them with churches for continued spiritual guidance. The mission of the Salvation Army is to proclaim the gospel of Christ, to persuade people to become His disciples, and to help meet the practical needs of humanity. Now in more than 100 countries, the Salvation Army continues to provide food, shelter, health care, education, rehabilitation, counseling, and disaster relief for the needy. In 1997, the Salvation Army served approximately 26 million people across the United States through its nearly 9,400 units of operation. For a more detailed picture of the Salvation Army's origins, read the life story of its co-founder in *Catherine Booth: A Biography* by Roger J. Green, chairperson of biblical and theological studies at Gordon College (Baker Books, 1996 – (800) 877-2665).

THE URBAN ALTERNATIVE

P.O. Box 4000
Dallas, TX 75208
Phone: (800) 800-3222
Fax: (214) 943-2632
E-mail: tua@flash.net
Website: www.tonyevans.org

The Urban Alternative, founded by Pastor Tony Evans, works to empower and equip churches to help meet the physical, spiritual, educational and economic needs of their communities. Its national ministries include Project Turnaround, a church consulting team that holds specialized seminars and provides individualized training for churches. The Urban Alternative also has a national Church Development Conference every fall for pastors, pastors' wives, and lay leaders, designed to equip the local church to have a greater influence on America's pressing social problems. This national ministry is a resource for Christian leaders committed to bringing Christ-centered solutions to bear on community problems.

WORLD VISION UNITED STATES

34834 Weyerhaeuser Way South
P.O. Box 9716
Federal Way, WA 98063-9716
Phone: (888) 511-6598
Website: www.worldvision.org

World Vision United States is a division of World Vision, the largest privately funded Christian relief and development organization in the world. World Vision USA programs include Churches at Work, Vision Cities, and Love INC.

Churches at Work, established in 1997 in response to welfare reform, is an on-line database of churches and faith-based organizations throughout the United States that are working to meet human needs in their communities. It was established to create a database for information sharing among churches about their best practices for local outreach. Ministry models can be located by topic or by geographical area. Churches at Work can be found at www.churchesat-work.org.

Vision Cities is World Vision's partnership with united ministries, churches, and organizations in specified cities. All the partners within a particular vision city share the goal of providing hope and assistance through Jesus Christ to families in urban communities. Vision Cities are located in Chicago; Los Angeles; Seattle/Tacoma; New York; Detroit; Washington, D.C.; and Minneapolis/St. Paul.

Love INC is a national organization of regional clearinghouses established by churches to connect with people in need, social services, and other area churches. For more information, see Chapter 8.

UNDERSTANDING WELFARE POLICY PAST AND PRESENT

AFDC was established in 1935 under the Social Security Act to provide support mainly to unemployed widows with children and to orphans. AFDC distributed cash aid to needy children who were deprived of parental support because a parent was deceased, absent from the home, out of work, or incapacitated. In the '60s and early '70s, AFDC was declared an entitlement. This meant that any family that qualified could receive cash assistance from its county welfare office (generally the county Department of Social Services) for as long as it qualified. Most persons with children qualified as long as they did not obtain a job that raised their income above the poverty line. The government policies that began in the Great Depression (the New Deal) and then mushroomed in the '60s (the Great Society) were intended to help families with children on a temporary basis.

WHAT WERE SOME OF THE NEGATIVE EFFECTS OF AFDC?

When President Lyndon Johnson announced the War on Poverty more than 30 years ago, he declared that this investment would repay society many times over. The result has been quite the opposite after 30 years of aggressive anti-poverty programs and 60 years of growth in government welfare spending. Government welfare,[109] including AFDC, encouraged dependency on the government, discouraged individual responsibility, and usurped the biblical roles of church and family. Government welfare also encouraged behaviors that directly correlate with a lifetime in poverty. Consider the return our country has received for nearly 7 trillion dollars in investments over the last 60 years:

THE EMERGENCE OF MULTIGENERATIONAL POVERTY

Children raised in families that receive welfare assistance are three times more likely to be on welfare when they become adults.[110]

AN INCREASE IN WELFARE DEPENDENCY

In 1996, one American child in seven was being raised on welfare. Poverty has increased, due in part to the strong anti-work effects of AFDC. A seven-year controlled study showed that each dollar of extra welfare money that an individual on welfare received decreased on average his or her concurrent work earnings by 80 percent.[111]

SKYROCKETING OUT-OF-WEDLOCK BIRTHS

When the War on Poverty began, the out-of-wedlock birth rate was one-quarter what it is today.[112] Under AFDC, a family's welfare benefit increased with each additional child.[113]

THE FOURFOLD INCREASE IN FATHERLESS FAMILIES

Over 19 million American children are growing up today in fatherless families, whereas in 1960, 5 million children lived in female-headed households.[114] Welfare has encouraged fathers, especially those who are unmarried, to abandon their responsibilities.

THE RISE IN WELFARE SPENDING

On average, the cost of the welfare system amounted to about $5,700 in taxes from each household that paid federal income tax in 1997.[115] Public-sector welfare spending in 1929 amounted to only $6.89 per person in 1997 dollars.[116] At the beginning of the War on Poverty, welfare spending absorbed roughly one percent of the total economy or gross domestic product (GDP). By 1993, welfare spending equaled 5.08 percent of the GDP, a level exceeding even the historical peak set during the Great Depression.[117]

THE ALARMING HIGH SCHOOL DROPOUT RATE

Young women raised in welfare-dependent families are two to three times less likely to graduate from high school than young women of similar race and socioeconomic backgrounds who were not raised on welfare.[118] Almost half of welfare mothers have not graduated from high school.[119]

THE ISOLATION OF THE POOREST FAMILIES

Welfare trapped a population in poverty, causing the poorest of the poor to remain in crumbling neighborhoods while the middle class moved to the suburbs. In 1920, city dwellers were a majority of the population; in 1970, more Americans were living in the suburbs than in cities, with the poorest of the poor still living in major cities with no way out.[120]

THE SUBURBANIZATION OF CHURCH OUTREACH

At the turn of the 20th century, the church was viewed as an urban institution. The city, including the "hard-core urban poor," was the church's domain.[121] Today, the bulk of church outreach within America focuses on the needs of the middle class rather than the poor. Many urban churches have moved to the suburbs, following the middle class.[122] Between 1946 and

1960, money spent on church building moved from $76 million to $1.6 billion — the bulk of which was spent on suburban church growth.[123]

THE DECLINE IN CHURCH BENEVOLENCE GIVING

Benevolence giving voluntary church funds that generally include local missions has been on the decline since the increase in government welfare programs. Benevolence giving per member as a percentage of personal income dropped from 0.66 percent in 1968 to 0.42 percent in 1994, a 37 percent decline.[124]

WHAT IS THE NEW PROGRAM THAT REPLACES AFDC, CALLED TEMPORARY ASSISTANCE TO NEEDY FAMILIES (TANF)?

The welfare reform law of 1996 reversed 60 years of social welfare policy.[125] It eliminated Aid to Families with Dependent Children (AFDC) and replaced it with a completely different program, Temporary Assistance to Needy Families (TANF).[126]

The reforms of 1996 are different from the Great Society and New Deal approach to poverty in two important areas. First, government responsibility has shifted from the federal government to the states.[127] The legislation now calls upon each state to experiment with the best way to help its poor move off cash assistance into gainful employment. The hope is that with more than 50 different experiments taking place,[128] the best government methods of helping the poor will emerge and be duplicated. Welfare reform has been called the most extensive experiment in reorganizing all levels of the U.S. government in the 20th century.[129]

Second, state collaboration with various community groups is vital in order to make this model successful. This includes collaboration with businesses, churches, and faith-based nonprofits. Speaking for President Clinton, then-Press Secretary Mike McCurry stated, "Everyone, in a sense, has roles to play in making welfare reform a success: the church, [the] community and those who are advocates on behalf of the children of America, the private sector, and certainly those elected officials with responsibilities like the President. Everybody has to be a part of the solution."[130]

Each state is required to comply with the following federal mandates under the new TANF program:

Require work in exchange for welfare cash benefits. TANF requires states to cut off those individuals who have been receiving welfare checks for two years and are not working. These individuals cannot receive any additional welfare checks until they are employed.[131] All states are required to have a two-year limit, and some states and counties have made these limits even shorter.

Reduce its welfare caseload. By the year 2000, each state must reduce its caseload by 40 percent. In the years following, the state must reduce its caseload by 5 percent more each year, to 50 percent in the year 2002. If a state fails to shrink its caseload by the required amount, those remaining on welfare must be engaged in work. Many are predicting that moving welfare recipients into work will become harder, not easier, as time goes on because most states have shrunk their caseloads by requiring those most employable to work first.[132]

Reduce out-of-wedlock births. This social trend alone has directly resulted from and contributed to the rise of welfare dependence and the breakdown of the family. TANF contains three provisions to combat out-of-wedlock births. First, it requires state governments to set numerical goals for reducing out-of-wedlock births in their states until 2008. Second, it provides bonus funding for states that reduce out-of-wedlock births without increasing abortion.[133] Third, it creates a new federally funded program for abstinence education.[134]

Eliminate cash assistance as an entitlement. Each state is required to limit a family's lifetime cash assistance benefit to five years.[135] This is perhaps the most radical change for welfare families, especially for those who have experienced generational poverty.

WHAT NEW FUNDING OPPORTUNITIES FOR CHURCHES AND FAITH-BASED MINISTRIES EXIST IN THE WELFARE REFORM LAW OF 1996?

A major feature of the new federal welfare legislation is its encouragement of state cooperation with faith-based charities and churches in serving needy families, called the Charitable Choice provision.[136]

According to Stanley W. Carlson-Thies of the Center for Public Justice:

> The Charitable Choice provision has three goals. First, it seeks to encourage states to expand the involvement of faith-based organizations and churches in the public anti-poverty effort. Second, through a range of measures it protects the religious integrity and character of faith-based organizations that are willing to accept government funds to provide services to the needy. Third, it safeguards the religious freedom of beneficiaries, both those who are willing to receive services from religious organizations and those who object to receiving services from such organizations.

> The Charitable Choice guidelines clarify and codify the constitutional requirements for governmental interaction with faith-based social-service providers. Too often constitutional law is misinterpreted as requiring that faith-based organizations be excluded from participation in governmental welfare programs or that their participation be conditioned on the removal of religious practices and symbols. Section 104 incorporates U.S. Supreme Court precedents for governmental neutrality between faith-based and secular providers of services, protection of the religious integrity of faith-based providers, and protection of the religious liberty of beneficiaries.[137]

Some of the rules of Charitable Choice are as follows:

Religious nonprofits and churches can either contract or receive vouchers for providing certain services to welfare recipients. The state or county cannot refuse to contract with them solely because of their religious character.

Religious nonprofits and churches can retain their religious character. They are not required to remove their religious art, icons, or other symbols.

Religious nonprofits and churches are permitted to continue their policies of hiring only employees who agree with their statements of faith.

Religious nonprofits and churches cannot refuse to help a participant who does not adhere to the beliefs of the church or nonprofit or who refuses to participate actively in a religious practice.

Welfare recipients have the right to choose religious or non-religious providers. They must be offered alternatives if their state or county has a contract with a religious nonprofit.

Whether or not a church or faith-based organization takes advantage of government funding available through the Charitable Choice provision is an individual decision for each ministry or congregation. Two primary benefits of the provision are that 1) it places government-based and faith-based social service providers on the same level, and 2) it will guarantee welfare recipients a choice of programs, including those that are faith-based, as they are exiting the welfare rolls.[138]

One of the main arguments against Charitable Choice is that Christian ministries will succumb to "mission creep,"[139] letting their mission statement change to mirror their funding sources, rather than their biblical objectives, over time. Churches and faith-based organizations in every circumstance must guard their Christian distinctives so that they offer something uniquely spiritual to the larger community.

It remains to be seen how the Charitable Choice provision will affect the social service community, the Christian community, and local and state governments. There are examples of churches and faith-based organizations using a principled approach even when receiving government money such as Charitable Choice. There are also examples of Christian ministries that have become less "Christian" over time as they have received government money. Both religious and secular organizations are watching the implementation of this provision, including such groups as the Center for Public Justice, the Christian Legal Society, People for the American Way, and the American Civil Liberties Union.

For a copy of the guidelines on Charitable Choice for your church, religious nonprofit, or county and state officials administering TANF funds, please contact the Center for Public Justice (see listing below). Also, *A Guide to Charitable Choice* can be accessed through their website at http://cpjustice.org/Cguide/Guide.html. You may also contact the Center for Public Justice for further assistance on how your church can be legally protected as you use government money available through the Charitable Choice provision.

THE CENTER FOR PUBLIC JUSTICE

P.O. Box 48368
Washington, DC 20002-0368
Phone: (410) 571-6300
Fax: (410) 571-6365
E-mail: inquiries@cpjustice.org
Website: http://cpjustice.org

The Center for Public Justice advocates justice for citizens of all faiths, and public policies that strengthen the institutions of civil society. To this end, the Center conducts public policy research and civic education from a Christian perspective. Executive Director James W. Skillen and Director of Social Policy Studies Stanley W. Carlson-Thies are the editors of *Welfare in America: Christian Perspectives on a Policy in Crisis (Eerdmans, 1996)*. With the Christian Legal Society, CPJ published the *Guide to Charitable Choice: The Rules of Section 104 of the 1996 Federal Welfare Law Governing State Cooperation with Faith-based Social-Service Providers*. The Tracking Charitable Choice Project, 1997-1999, is directed by Stanley Carlson-Thies. This project is studying how nine states (California, Illinois, Massachusetts, Michigan, Mississippi, New York, Texas, Virginia, and Wisconsin) have changed their practices and policies in order to implement Charitable Choice. Faith-based organizations in those states are also being surveyed to determine whether Charitable Choice has made a difference to their programs.

THE HERITAGE FOUNDATION

214 Massachusetts Avenue, NE
Washington, DC 20002-4999
Phone: (202) 546-4400
Fax: (202) 546-8328
Website: www.townhall.com/heritage

The Heritage Foundation (THF) is a research and educational institute that formulates and promotes public policies based on the principles of free enterprise, limited government, individual freedom, traditional American values, and a strong national defense. THF has produced numerous reports on welfare reform, including the seminal work by Robert Rector and William F. Lauber titled *America's Failed $5.4 Trillion War on Poverty* (1995). THF publishes the bimonthly magazine *Policy Review*.

In cooperation with other conservative organizations, THF hosts Breakfast for Champions, a series of bimonthly breakfasts to raise money for community groups that work with low-income Washington, D.C., residents. Organizations that have benefited include The Washington Scholarship Fund, Gospel Rescue Ministries, Northwest Crisis Pregnancy Center, Saturday Learning Extension Program, Clean and Sober Streets, and Prison Fellowship Ministries.

THE WELFARE INFORMATION NETWORK

1000 Vermont Avenue, NW
Suite 600
Washington, DC 20005
Phone: (202) 628-5790
Fax: (202) 628-4206
E-mail: welfinfo@welfareinfo.org
Website: www.welfareinfo.org

The Welfare Information Network (WIN) is a foundation-funded Internet clearinghouse project to help states and communities obtain the information, policy analysis, and technical assistance they need to develop and implement welfare reforms. The WIN website is updated weekly. It summarizes the information and technical assistance resources available in some 40 to 45 program and issue areas. These areas include faith-based involvement, child care, domestic violence, substance abuse, immigrants, and pregnancy prevention. The site also includes summaries of federal welfare legislation; a catalog of and links to other welfare-related web sites; a calendar of welfare-related events; and links to more than 2,700 organizations' and publications' web pages containing program information, policy analysis, legislative information, and "best practices." The site provides links to state agency sites and to electronic versions of state TANF plans. A "Hot Topics" page highlights recent publications, planned research and evaluation activities, and discussions of emerging issues. WIN maintains a clearinghouse on program and management issues, including faith-based involvement and agency organization and reorganization.

Afterword

by Gary L. Bauer

Practical Christian obedience … comes [not] from the backward gaze of gratitude. …
[I]t comes from the forward gaze of faith.[140]
John Piper, senior pastor, Bethlehem Baptist Church, Minneapolis, Minn.

W e are at the turn of a century. The last time a century turned, it was well known that churches were a vital lifeline to uplift the poor. They were providing the vision and inspiration for the country in helping those most in need in our communities. Mary Richmond, a well-known Christian worker with the poor, wrote in 1899:

> After all has been said in objection to past and present methods of church charity, we must realize that, if the poor are to be effectually helped by charity, the inspiration must come from the church. The church has always been and will continue to be the chief source of charitable energy; and I believe that, to an increasing degree, the church will be the leader in charitable experiment and in the extension of the scope of charitable endeavor. … [T]he church has always been the pioneer in such work.[141]

Even as the clock struck midnight on January 1, 1901, the *New York Journal* noted that America's concern for its neighbors had grown. This was one of the markings of the century that had just concluded.

> Perhaps the most remarkable of all the characteristic developments of the nineteenth century has been the growth of human sympathy. The feeling that every man is really his brother's keeper has become stronger than ever before.[142]

The verdict is still out on what the next century will be like. This is the moment for churches to demonstrate commitment to the poor again. Welfare reform provides a window of opportunity for churches to demonstrate Christlike love and hope to the country.

In this hour, the church must reclaim biblical charity. We must bring new solutions to bear on our nation's most pressing social problems, particularly long-term welfare dependency. We must recognize that it is not enough to give money to the poor; we must give ourselves. We must ask ourselves: Are we throwing money at people, perpetuating the welfare state mentality, or are we helping to transform lives that can then testify to the restoration found only in God's love? Are we truly loving our neighbors?

The 21st century could be the century when each church is more courageous, more creative, and more compassionate in loving the poor in America. Imagine if each church in America opened its doors wider to the orphans and widows of today, including welfare mothers and their children – our churches would change, our needy communities would change, and ultimately, our country would change for the better.

Let it be said that this will be the century when the church will step out in faith and minister more courageously to the strangers, aliens, widows, orphans, and prisoners in our communities. May we see many more families in America delivered forever from the captivity of poverty. May we see many more churches restored as we seek the welfare of our neighbors in need.

December 1998

Left to right: **Gary Bauer, with Scott Dimmock, Nikki Davidson and Sammie Morrison of the Southeast White House, a Christ-centered ministry house in Washington, D.C.**

Gary L. Bauer served as president of Family Research Council from 1988 to January 1999. Formerly, Mr. Bauer worked for President Reagan as the undersecretary of the Department of Education and as assistant to President Reagan for policy development and director of the Office of Policy Development. He is the author of three books, *Children at Risk: The Battle for the Hearts and Minds of Our Kids* (1990), written with Dr. James C. Dobson; *Our Journey Home* (1992); and *Our Hopes, Our Dreams* (1996). Mr. Bauer, who grew up in a blue-collar town in Kentucky, is an internationally known spokesman for the family.

Endnotes

1 Attributed.

2 Personal conversation with Mike Doyle, executive director of Cornerstone Assistance Ministries, the ministry among the poor that he founded. *See* Chapter 8 for more information.

3 In fiscal year 1996, the national AFDC caseload averaged about 4.6 million families a month. This was before the 1996 congressional reforms. The number of people (adults and children combined) on welfare fell 37 percent, from 14.1 million in January 1993 to 8.9 million in March 1998. Twenty-seven percent of that drop has occurred since August 1996. *See* Mark V. Nadel, associate director, Income Security Issues, United States Health, Education, and Human Services Division, *Welfare Reform: States Are Restructuring Programs to Reduce Welfare Dependence* (Washington, D.C.: GAO, June 1998), pp. 14, 97.

4 In July 1996, the income eligibility limit for a three-person family in the first month of earnings ranged from $370 per month in Alabama to $1,220 in California. Jerome L. Gallagher, Megan Gallagher, Kevin Perese, Susan Schreiber, and Keith Watson, *One Year after Federal Welfare Reform: A Description of State Temporary Assistance for Needy Families (TANF) Decisions as of October 1997* (Washington, D.C.: The Urban Institute, 1998), pp. 7-9.

5 In 1996, there were 9,469,000 children in AFDC families. That's about 14 percent of all children.

6 Jason DeParle, "Getting Opal Caples to Work," *The New York Times Magazine,* August 24, 1997, Sec. 6:33, p. 60.

7 Source: Quarterly Public Assistance Statistics.

8 1993 AFDC Statistic (Source: Statistical Assessment Service).

9 *Ibid.*

10 *Ibid.*

11 *Ibid.*

12 *Ibid.*

13 Of the nearly 5 million families on AFDC in 1994, half were on it for over 10 years. For many, though, the stay is short and can mean going on and off AFDC intermittently. It is difficult to "average" out the typical stay on welfare. (Source: Statistical Assessment Service.) For a clear discussion of this difficult topic, *see* Mary Jo Bane

and David T. Ellwood, *Welfare Realities: From Rhetoric to Reform* (Cambridge: Harvard University Press, 1994), chapter 2.

14   While African-Americans are 13 percent of the total population, they make up 37 percent of the total welfare caseload. Hispanics are 11 percent of the total population and make up 22 percent of the total welfare caseload. Source: Bruce Katz, Senior Fellow at the Brookings Institution, *Welfare Reform in the Cities*, Presentation to the National Summit on Churches and Welfare Reform, Brookings Center on Urban and Metropolitan Policy, February 1, 1999. There are various reasons why welfare dependency has so deeply affected minority families, including racism, corporate sin, and church abdication of local outreach.

15   *Central cities* are defined to include any city or county that meets the definition of metropolitan city or urban county under HUD's community development block grant program. This includes but is not limited to New York, Chicago, Los Angeles, Philadelphia, Detroit, Houston, Baltimore, Dallas, Cleveland, Indianapolis, Milwaukee, San Francisco, San Diego, San Antonio, Boston, Memphis, St. Louis, New Orleans, Columbus, and Washington, D.C.

16   Jason DeParle, "Welfare Rolls Show Growing Racial and Urban Imbalance," *The New York Times*, July 27, 1998, p. A1.

17   Names have been changed.

18   Name has been changed.

19   Dietrich Bonhoeffer, *Life Together* (San Francisco: Harper & Row, 1954), p. 38. Translated and with an introduction by John W. Doberstein.

20   Interview conducted by Marie Rapier, former FRC Witherspoon Fellow and college roommate of Viera.

21   For more information, *see* Viv Grigg, *Companion to the Urban Poor* (Monrovia, Calif.: MARC, 1990). Ordering information is in Chapter 10.

22   Matthew 25:31-32 notes that this passage refers to a nation caring for the needy, rather than one individual caring for another.

23   Personal conversation with Beverly Baumann, a former welfare recipient who is now on staff at her church, Heritage Christian Center, as the director of graphics/ editing for its monthly newspaper, *The Heritage Happenings*. *See* Chapter Five for more information on Heritage Christian Center.

24   Personal conversation with Mike Herman. Mike and his wife, Tonya, are members of Calvary Baptist Church of Compton, Calif., and staff members of Here's Life Inner City, a Ministry of Campus Crusade for Christ. *See* Chapter 9 for information on Here's Life Inner City.

25   Personal interview conducted by Marie Rapier.

26   *Ibid.*

27   Attributed.

28   Richard Wolf, "Law lets states increase churches' welfare role," *USA Today*, October 9, 1997, p. A1.

29   The Personal Responsibility and Work Opportunity Reconciliation Act of 1996, H.R. 3734, 104th Congress, 2d Session, P.L. 104-193.

30   PRWORA replaced four existing cash assistance programs and related welfare programs – Aid to Families with Dependent Children (AFDC); AFDC Administration;

Job Opportunities and Basic Skills (JOBS); and the Emergency Assistance Program – with the Temporary Assistance for Needy Families (TANF) block grant.

31 There are certain exemptions and modifications for two-parent families or one-parent families with young children. There is also an exemption possible for 20 percent of the total welfare roll to allow for cases of extreme hardship (*see* Appendix, notes 132, 135).

32 Franklin D. Roosevelt, speech delivered Jan. 4, 1935.

33 Linda Burton, Andrew J. Cherlin, Judith Francis, Robin Jarrett, James Quane, Constance Williams, N. Michelle Stem Cook, *What Welfare Recipients and the Fathers of Their Children Are Saying about Welfare Reform*, June 1998, p. 5. This is the first report from a larger project, "Welfare Reform and Children: A Three-City Study." This report is on 15 focus group discussions in Baltimore, Boston, and Chicago.

34 Twenty-seven percent of American children are growing up today in fatherless families. In 1996, there were 9,855,000 single-parent homes headed by a mother only. Over 19 million children under age 18 live in mother-only families. Source: 1996 Census, "Current Population Report."

35 In 1920, 3 percent of American children were born out of wedlock; in 1991, that figure was 30 percent. In 1920, approximately 12 percent of African-American children were born out of wedlock; in 1991, that figure had risen to 68 percent. Gertrude Himmelfarb, *The De-Moralization of Society: From Victorian Virtues to Modern Values* (New York: Alfred A. Knopf, 1995), pp. 223-224.

36 Benevolence giving is the voluntary church fund that generally includes local missions. Gustav Niebuhr, "Evangelical Protestants Giving Less to Churches, Study Says," *The New York Times*, December 9, 1997, late ed., p. A22. The study cited in the article is titled, "The State of Church Giving Through 1995." For more information contact Empty Tomb, Inc., Champaign, Illinois.

37 Harvie M. Conn, *The American City and the Evangelical Church: A Historical Overview* (Grand Rapids: Baker Books, 1994), pp. 84, 99-100.

38 Testimony of Richard P. Nathan before the Human Resources Subcommittee of the House Ways and Means Committee, Washington, D.C., March 19, 1998.

39 The welfare reform legislation took effect for all states on July 1, 1997. Some state plans started earlier.

40 States are allowed to make exceptions for 20 percent of welfare recipients to allow for those who have extreme hardships (*see* Appendix, note 132), but almost no one else can receive federal welfare payments for more than five years in a lifetime.

41 These include Mississippi's Faith and Families Initiative, South Carolina's Putting Families First Initiative, and Michigan's Project Zero/Good Samaritan Ministries Initiative. *See* Chapter 8.

42 Then-Governor Kirk Fordice of Mississippi as quoted by Jason DeParle in "Welfare Reform's First Months – A Special Report: Success, and Frustration, as Welfare Rules Change," *New York Times*, Dec. 30, 1997.

43 Amy Sherman, "Little Miracles: How Churches Are Responding to Welfare Reform," *The American Enterprise*, Jan.- Feb. 1998, p. 68. Bill Raymond is the former executive director of Good Samaritan Ministries. *See* Chapter 8 for more information.

44 Sacramento County Welfare Director Cheryl Davis as quoted by Don Lattin in "On the Crusade's Front Lines: Congregations add support, community concern to job-training mix," *The San Francisco Chronicle,* September 16, 1998, p. A1.

45 Loren Snippe, the welfare director for Ottawa County, Michigan, as quoted by Don Lattin in "On the Crusade's Front Lines," *ibid.*

46 Hundreds of millions of dollars are being spent studying the success of welfare reform. Groups conducting these studies include the Urban Institute, the U.S. Census Bureau, and the Manpower Demonstration Research Corporation.

47 Governor David M. Beasley, "Governor Challenges All to do Their Share to Ensure S.C. Works," *The Post and Courier,* May 15, 1997, Section A, p. 15.

48 Ottawa County, Mich., was the first county in the country to reduce its welfare caseload to zero as a part of Governor John Engler's Project Zero initiative. Governor Engler attributed much of its success to the active involvement of churches. *See* Jon Jeter, "A Homespun Safety Net: Michigan Community Finds Jobs for All on Welfare," *The Washington Post*, October 8, 1997, late ed., p. A1.

49 *Ibid. See* Good Samaritan Ministries in Chapter 8.

50 Timothy J. Keller, *Ministries of Mercy* (Phillipsburg, N.J.: P & R Publishing, 1997), p. 175. *See* Chapter 10 for ordering information on *Ministries of Mercy*.

51 Personal conversation with Rita Bright.

52 Personal conversation with Leslie Carbone.

53 See Phil Reed, "Toward a Theology of Christian Community Development," Chapter 2, *Restoring At-Risk Communities: Doing it Together & Doing It Right,* John M. Perkins, ed. (Grand Rapids: Baker Books, 1995), pp. 30-31.

54 *Ibid.*

55 Rita Bright is the neighborhood outreach leader and community organizer for Belmont Street Community in the Columbia Heights neighborhood of Washington, D.C. Her calling is to restore her community just as she has been restored.

56 James Edwin Orr, *Evangelical Awakening, 1900-Onward* (Chicago: Moody Press, 1975), Second Edition, Introduction, p. 7. The late James Edwin Orr is known as one of the foremost authorities on spiritual awakening in the 20th century. He introduced Billy Graham to a direct encounter with the Holy Spirit before Graham's 1949 crusade in Los Angeles.

57 Name has been changed.

58 Name has been changed.

59 Name has been changed.

60 For a copy of the transcript and/or video of this meeting, contact Pastor Debbie Stafford or Pastor Dave McFann at Project Heritage, Denver, Colorado. *See* Chapter Five for contact information.

61 Commissioner John Brackney at the Welfare Reform Roundtable, March 26, 1998, hosted by Heritage Christian Center, Project Heritage and Family Research Council. Colorado has devolved control of welfare to the county level. Commissioner Brackney serves on Colorado Counties, Inc., Legislative Committee and Health and Human Services Committee. He also serves on the National Association of Counties Human Services and Education Committee and Welfare and Social Services Subcommittee.

62 Personal conversation.

63 Henri Nouwen, *Can You Drink the Cup?* (Notre Dame, Ind.: Ave Maria Press, 1996), p. 46. Henri Nouwen was the pastor of L'Arche Daybreak Community in Toronto, where he shared his life with people with mental disabilities.

64 Personal conversation with Becky Wellford. Becky has been ministering in the inner city of Richmond, Va., for the last 11 years through Victory Life Fellowship and STEP (see Chapter Eight for information on STEP).

65 Personal conversation with Edith Jones.

66 Personal conversations with Clark and Edith Jones. Edith Jones' testimony includes bringing together over 380 Washington, D.C., ministries to work together for the poor. Clark Jones is the Executive Director of CityTeam Ministries in Chester, Pa.

67 Sunday morning in many communities is still one of the most segregated days of the week. Only five of every 100 African-Americans belong to a majority-white Protestant denomination. The number of whites who belong to a majority-black denomination is even smaller. Spencer Perkins and Chris Rice, *More Than Equals: Racial Healing for the Sake of the Gospel* (Downers Grove, Ill.: InterVarsity Press, 1993), p. 60.

68 Virgil Gulker (the executive director of Kids/Hope/USA, a national church-based after-school mentoring program for public school children, based in Holland, Mich.,), quoted in *A World Without Welfare*, David Wagner, ed., (Washington, D.C.: Family Research Council, 1997), pp. 110, 111.

69 Donald Dayton, *Discovering an Evangelical Heritage* (Hendrickson Publishers, Inc., 1976) 115-116 (out of print); also http://www.iugm.org/mcauley.html. The International Union of Gospel Missions was organized on September 17, 1913, in New York City. It currently has 250 member rescue missions around the world. *See* Chapter 10 for more information.

70 Norris Magnuson, *Salvation in the Slums: Evangelical Social Work*, 1865-1920 (Grand Rapids: The Scarecrow Press, 1977), pp. 79-82 (out of print).

71 Viv Grigg, op. cit., p. 22.

72 The Azusa Street Revival of 1906 is known as the beginning of the Pentecostal Movement. *See* Wellington Boone, *Breaking Through: Taking the Kingdom into the Culture by Out-Serving Others* (Nashville: Broadman and Holman Publishers, 1996), pp. 56-57, 87.

73 Robert Metcalf, former director of social services for the state of Virginia, has defined these as "core job readiness skills."

74 Heritage Christian Center in Denver, Colo., has started various support groups that are accessible to low-income individuals and families. Ask for a copy of their *Support Groups Guide* (*see* Chapter Five for contact information).

75 Some churches use Ron Blue's or Larry Burkett's personal finance and budgeting materials.

76 Oak Cliff Bible Fellowship in Dallas, Texas, has developed a good relationship with a temporary agency in Dallas. The agency has been able to find employment for 70 percent of the graduates from the church's alternative education center. Oak Cliff Bible Fellowship is connected with the Urban Alternative (*see* Chapter Ten for contact information).

77 Many businesses are more willing to hire welfare recipients if they have references and ongoing support from churches.

78 See U.S. Department of Justice, INS, Form I-9, "Employment Eligibility Verification" for required documents for employment.

79 America's Promise, The Alliance for Youth in Alexandria, Virginia, has developed materials for employers interested in starting a "Job Shadow Day."

80 *See* the entry on the Washington Project, a church-based basic business training and small loan program to help welfare recipients start their own businesses, in Chapter Eight.

81 In general, workers are eligible for the credit if they earned less than $10,030 without a qualifying child; less than $26,473 with one qualifying child; or less than $30,095 with more than one qualifying child. The maximum credit available on 1998 returns is $2,271 for parents with one child; $3,756 for those with two or more children; and $341 for childless workers.

82 D.R.E.A.M. Ministry of Fresno, Cal., utilizes Fresno Christian businessmen and women to teach Hmong and Laotian refugees vocational skills to obtain full-time employment.

83 A vast number of legal immigrants receiving welfare benefits are non-English speaking. Heritage Christian Center in Denver, Colo., uses Hooked on Phonics as its literacy curriculum.

84 Businesses may be eligible for tax credits if they hire welfare recipients. *See* Tate & Tyron, Certified Public Accountants, "Credit Where Credit Is Due: The 1997 Tax Law & Your Family" (Washington, D.C.: Family Research Council, 1998), p. 30.

85 Church-based day care centers that receive government vouchers can still teach children about Christ. *See* the appendix on the Charitable Choice provision of the '96 welfare law. You can contact your state's child care licensing agency to obtain a license, and contact your state or county department of human/social services to learn how your church-based day-care center can accept vouchers from welfare mothers who need child care in order to go to work. Also, *see Vouchers for Christian Child Care fact sheet* (FX507) available from Focus on the Family, Colorado Springs, Colo. (*see* Appendix, notes 138).

86 Kids Care in Minneapolis/St. Paul asks area churches to provide funds (approximately $200) for the start-up supplies required by child care licensing to start a home-based child-care center. In 1998, churches helped 65 low-income women get their businesses started by providing the funding for cribs, high chairs, fire extinguishers, smoke detectors, and first-aid kits.

87 The Cooperating Congregations of Greater Waukesha, Wis., runs A-Hand-To-Hold Day Care Center. It was founded in January 1998 primarily to address these unique child care needs. (*See The Milwaukee Journal Sentinel,* February 24, 1998, p. 1.)

88 Most day care centers do not accept a child with any kind of illness.

89 Bridges to Work in Denver, Colo., is a program that places participants in suburban jobs and provides transportation for them to and from work for 18 months. Many welfare recipients have a "reverse commute," where they live in the city and their employers are located in the suburbs. Often their bus commutes are

complicated and lengthy.

90 Check with your local transportation system to see whether they offer discount tokens for nonprofit organizations.

91 Heritage Christian Center in Denver, Colo., and Willow Creek Community Church in Barrington, Ill., have regular car clinics at their church. Skilled men or women in the church volunteer their time to perform car repairs for financially struggling parents. The Good News Garage, a ministry started by three Lutheran churches in Burlington, provides donated cars and car repair at cost to welfare families with jobs, or prospective jobs, who need transportation to work. Charity Cars in Orlando, Fla., takes donated cars, repairs them, and gives them to welfare recipients. The welfare recipients must find jobs within 30 days in order to keep the cars.

92 Volunteer mechanics at Willow Creek Community Church in Barrington, Ill., fix up used cars donated by church members and give them to families in need. In 1996, 600 cars were repaired and distributed, often to single mothers who could not accept job offers without transportation.

93 Kingdom Cars in Fort Mill, SC., asks used car dealers to donate cars for transitioning welfare recipients. The first woman who received a used car through this ministry gave it to another transitioning welfare recipient when she was on her feet.

94 In Lexington County, Ky. churches are asked by social services to donate vans to provide vanpooling for welfare recipients to their jobs.

95 In Manchester, Tenn., Baptist and Methodist churches bus welfare clients and their children to church for mentoring programs.

96 In Birmingham, Ala., area businessmen contracted with a local bus service to pick up newly employed welfare recipients and take them to their jobs.

97 Your local phone company can set up a block of voice mailboxes for your church to provide to individuals needing to receive employment-related messages.

98 Faith Communities in Action in northern Virginia has published a comprehensive directory of services offered by the faith-based community. This is an extremely valuable resource that churches can give to social workers helping transitioning welfare families.

99 Santa Clara County in California started JOB KEEPER in October 1997. It is a 24-hour hotline for welfare recipients to call if they have transportation or child care problems, or if there are crises preventing them from getting to or staying at work.

100 *See* the NIV Recovery Devotional Bible (Zondervan Publishing: Grand Rapids, Michigan, 1993), p. 1436, for a listing of Christian recovery groups.

101 Each church is responsible to house, feed and transport families to and from work and appointments if needed. Children remain in their schools. Support teams at each church work to help develop community connections to stabilize the family. Contact the National Interfaith Hospitality Network in Summit, N.J., for more information.

102 Contact Heritage Christian Center/Project Heritage in Denver, Colo., for more information on developing this type of ministry (*see* Chapter Five for contact information).

103 The Community Outreach Center in Bel Air, Md., has developed the Loan Up Program. Accepted individuals are loaned up to $300 interest-free and given financial management training. The Loan Up Program teaches fiscal responsibility and demonstrates procedures for obtaining funds.

104 *See* Chapter 10 for ordering information. Dr. Sherman is a nationally known speaker and writer on church outreach to welfare families. She is director of urban ministries at Trinity Presbyterian Church, Charlottesville, Va.

105 This is the website for the Washington, D.C., affiliate.

106 Contact Scott Manly, executive director of Cornerstone Assistance Network of Oklahoma City, at (405) 557-1811. It was started in November 1996.

107 Contact Chris Beech, executive director of Tulsa Cornerstone Assistance Network, at (918) 587-0224. It was initiated in January 1997.

108 26 Love INC affiliates have web pages. This web page is for the affiliate in Indianapolis, Indiana.

109 Government welfare, according to Robert Rector, a policy analyst at the Heritage Foundation, is "the total set of government programs — federal and state — that are designed explicitly to assist poor and low-income Americans."

110 M. Anne Hill and June O'Neill, *Underclass Behaviors in the United States: Measurement and Analysis of Determinants* (New York: City University of New York, Baruch College, March 1990), as cited by Robert Rector and William F. Lauber in *America's Failed $5.4 Trillion War on Poverty* (Washington, D.C.: The Heritage Foundation, 1995), p. 25.

111 Robert Rector, "Welfare: Expanding the Reform," Chapter 7 in *Issues '98: The Candidate's Briefing Book*, Stuart M. Butler and Kim R. Holmes, eds. (Washington, D.C.: Heritage Foundation, 1998). The SIME/DIME (Seattle/Denver Income Maintenance Experiment) experiment that was conducted between 1971 and 1978 showed the strong anti-work effects of cash assistance programs.

112 *See* Chapter 3, note 35.

113 Under AFDC, states would increase the welfare benefit with each additional child. Under TANF, states can choose to implement a family cap policy for welfare benefits.

114 1996 Census, "Current Population Report." *See* note 34.

115 Between 1965 and 1997, welfare spending cost taxpayers $6.98 trillion (in constant 1997 dollars). In fiscal year 1997, total federal and state spending on welfare programs was $407.2 billion, of which 23.3 percent was cash aid. (Robert Rector, "Welfare: Expanding the Reform," *op. cit.*) During fiscal year 1996, over $20 billion in combined federal and state spending was cash assistance paid into the national combined welfare caseload.

116 Robert Rector, "Welfare: Expanding the Reform," Chapter 7, *op. cit.*

117 Rector and Lauber, *America's Failed $5.4 Trillion War on Poverty, op. cit.*

118 Robert Rector "Welfare: Expanding the Reform," Chapter 7, *op. cit.*

119 Bureau of the Census, "Current Population Report," 1993.

120 Forty-three percent of the very poor, which are those families who have a total family income less than one-half of the poverty threshold, live in central cities. Joseph Dalaker and Mary Naifeh, U.S. Bureau of the Census, Current Population Reports, P60-201, *Poverty in the US: 1997* (Washington, D.C.: United States

Government Printing Office, 1998), Table 2, p. 7. See note 15.

121 Harvie M. Conn, *The American City and the Evangelical Church: A Historical Overview* (Grand Rapids: Baker Books, 1994), pp. 99-100. The white middle class was the first group that could afford to leave the city and establish communities at a safe distance from the problems of the urban neighborhoods. Following the white population, a majority of both the African-American and Hispanic middle class found their way to suburban communities, "leaving behind the hard-core urban poor."

122 The "suburban shift" reached its peak between 1945 and 1970. *Ibid.*, p. 84.

123 Winthrop S. Hudson, *Religion in America*, Second Edition (New York: Charles Scribner's Sons, 1973), pp. 382, as cited by Harvie M. Conn, in *The American City and the Evangelical Church: A Historical Overview, op. cit.*, p. 97.

124 Gustav Niebuhr, "Evangelical Protestants Giving Less to Churches, Study Says," *The New York Times,* Dec. 9, 1997, late ed., p. A22. Part of a larger study titled "The State of Church Giving Through 1995." For more information contact Empty Tomb, Inc., Champaign, Ill.

125 Over 75 federal welfare programs remain unchanged, however.

126 The welfare reform law replaced four existing cash assistance and related welfare programs (Aid to Families with Dependent Children (AFDC); AFDC Administration; Job Opportunities and Basic Skills (JOBS); and the Emergency Assistance Program) with a new block grant to states called the Temporary Assistance for Needy Families (TANF) block grant. (House Republican Conference Summary, #104-7, June 19, 1996, Personal Responsibility and Work Opportunity Reconciliation Act, H.R. 3734, H. Rept. 104-725.)

127 Through a block grant, money is provided by the federal government to another governmental structure for a broad, flexible purpose to serve a general population with varying needs; e.g., the new welfare block grant called TANF, effective July 1, 1997.

128 Some states have even devolved their welfare programs to the county level.

129 Steven Hayward, "The Shocking Success of Welfare Reform," *Policy Review* Jan.-Feb. 1998, p. 10: "Welfare reform is the most extensive experiment in federalism in the 20th century."

130 White House Press Secretary Mike McCurry, M2 Presswire, Washington, D.C., Jan. 7, 1997.

131 In order for cash assistance beneficiaries to be considered as engaged in work activities, single parents must participate in at least 20 hours per week of approved work activities. That requirement increases to 30 hours by FY 2000. There are certain exemptions and modifications for two-parent families or single-parent families with young children. States are allowed to exempt 20 percent of their case-load from the two-year time limit.

132 The harder cases to move off welfare will be the states' target as they near the year 2002. This will include those who are a product of generational poverty, those with drug and alcohol addictions, those with little to no education, those with no work history, and those without English skills.

133 The U.S. Department of Health and Human Services is required to rank the states annually on the basis of their reductions in out-of-wedlock births among families

receiving TANF assistance and will award bonuses to up to five states for reductions in out-of-wedlock births among the general population.

134 The federal reform law included a provision to enhance states' efforts to provide sexual abstinence education and authorized $50 million annually for this purpose. States can use this money only for the development of mentoring, counseling, and adult supervision programs that encourage abstinence. As of June 1998, all 50 states had applied for these funds with proposals to initiate new programs or expand upon existing efforts that focus on abstinence.

135 The welfare reform law took effect for all states on July 1, 1997. Some state plans started earlier. The new welfare policies guarantee welfare benefits for only a total of five years for each family. There is an exemption possible for 20 percent of the total welfare caseload for cases of extreme hardship. These cases, determined by each state, can include parents with disabled children, women recovering from domestic violence, substance abusers in recovery, and those who cannot work due to a debiltating condition.

136 Section 104 of the Personal Responsibility and Work Opportunity Reconciliation Act of 1996, H.R. 3734, 104th Congress, 2D Session, P.L. 104-193.

137 From the Introduction to *A Guide to Charitable Choice* (Washington, D.C.: The Center for Public Justice, and Annandale, Va.: The Center for Law and Religious Freedom, 1997), p. 1. Reprinted with permission of Stanley W. Carlson-Thies, director, Project on Government and the Religious Social Sector, The Center for Public Justice, Washington, D.C. *A Guide to Charitable Choice* is accessible at http://cpjustice.org.

138 Child-care services for poor families are administered under a different program with different rules (Child Care and Development Block Grant program, begun in 1990). When welfare families pay for their child care by using vouchers, they may seek services from any provider the state has licensed, which can include explicitly Bible-centered programs operated in churches. But when states contract with programs to provide child-care services, then those programs are subject to many rules that water down their religious content.

139 See Chapter 3 of *Seducing the Samaritan* by Joe Loconte (Boston, Mass.: Pioneer Institute for Public Policy, 1997).

140 John Piper, *Future Grace* (Sisters, Ore.: Multnomah Books, 1995), p. 43.

141 Mary Richmond, *Friendly Visiting Among the Poor* (Montclair, N.J.: Patterson Smith, 1899), pp. 174-175 (out of print). Mary Richmond is the founder of modern social work.

142 *New York Journal,* January 1, 1901, editorial page; quoted by Marvin Olasky in *The Tragedy of American Compassion* (Washington, D.C.: Regnery, 1992), p. 135.